PRAYING WITH YOUR
WHOLE HEART

Praying with
your Whole Heart

ST. AUGUSTINE
ST. CATHERINE OF SIENA
AN ANONYMOUS MONK
OF FOURTEENTH-CENTURY ENGLAND
THOMAS À KEMPIS

PARACLETE PRESS
BREWSTER, MASSACHUSETTS

2014 First printing

Praying with Your Whole Heart

ISBN 978-1-61261-507-3

Consists of excerpts from material previously published by Paraclete Press, Inc.

The Paraclete Press name and logo (dove on cross) are trademarks of Paraclete Press, Inc.

Cover Art by Sharon France. Sharon's original paintings can be found at: www.francegallery.net

Library of Congress Cataloging-in-Publication Data is available.

10 9 8 7 6 5 4 3 2 1

Published by Paraclete Press
Brewster, Massachusetts
www.paracletepress.com

Printed in the United States of America

CONTENTS

BRIEF BIOGRAPHIES OF THE CONTRIBUTORS

FOREWORD

This is a deceptively simple book, written by four experts on the Christian spiritual life. Each of them writes with clarity and from a great depth of personal experience, and yet what each describes is something that is ultimately beyond description. That's what we mean by the book being deceptively simple: you cannot obtain what they describe by simply reading.

This is a collection of four distinct but united voices on the subject of how to pray, and how to reach a new level in your prayer life. In these pages, you will meet some of the most passionate Christians in the history of our faith: St. Augustine of Hippo, St. Catherine of Siena, an anonymous English monk of the fourteenth century, and Thomas à Kempis. Their viewpoints are presented chronologically, and short biographies of each may be found at the conclusion of the book.

ST. AUGUSTINE

From *The Confessions*

"STARTING FROM A RESTLESS HEART"
From *The Confessions*, book XIII, 1, 3, 8

BOOK I
Infancy to Age Fifteen

ONE

You are great, O Lord, and greatly to be praised. Great is your power, and your wisdom is infinite.[1] And man would praise you; man, who is but a small particle of your creation; yes, man, though he carries with him his mortality, the evidence of his sin, the evidence that you resist the proud; yet man, but a particle of your creation, would praise you.[2]

You awake us to delight in your praise; for you made us for yourself, and our hearts are restless until they rest in you.

Grant me, Lord, to know and understand which of these is most important, to call on you or to praise you. And again, to know you or to call on you. For who can call on you without knowing you? For he who does not know you may call on you as other than you are. Or perhaps we call on you that we may know you? *But how shall they call on him in whom they have not believed? or how shall they believe without a preacher?* And *they who seek the Lord shall praise him.* For they that seek shall find him, and those who find shall praise him. Let me seek you, Lord, by calling on you, and call on you believing in you, for you have been preached to us. My faith calls on you, Lord, the faith you have given me, the faith you have breathed into me through the incarnation of your Son, through the ministry of the preacher.[3]

TWO

But how shall I call upon my God, my God and Lord? For when I call on him, I ask him to come into myself. And what room is there in me, where my God can come—God who made heaven and earth? Is there anything in me, O Lord my God, that can contain you? Indeed, do heaven and earth which you have made, and in which you made me, contain you? Or, since nothing could exist without you, does every existing thing contain you? Why, then, do I ask that you come into me, since I, too, exist—I who could not exist if you were not in me? Why do I say this? Because even if I were in hell, yet you would be there also. For *if I go down into hell, you are there.* I could not exist then, O my God, could not exist at all, unless you were in me. Or should I not rather say, I could not exist unless I were in you, *from whom are all things, by whom are all things, and in whom are all things.*

Even so, Lord, even so. Where do I call you to come, since I am in you? Or whence can you enter into me? For where beyond heaven and earth could I go that my God might come there into me, who has said, *I fill the heaven and the earth?*

THREE

Do the heaven and earth then contain you, since you fill them? Or do you fill them and yet overflow, since they cannot contain you? And where, when the heaven and earth are filled, do you pour forth that which remains of yourself? Or indeed, is there no need that you who contain all things should be contained by anything, since those things you fill, you fill by containing them? For the vessels that you fill do not sustain you, since even if they were broken, you would not be poured out. And when you are poured out on us, you are not cast down, but we are uplifted. You are not dissipated, but we are drawn together. But as you fill all things, do you fill them with your whole self, or, since all things cannot contain you wholly, do they contain part of you? Do they all contain the same part at once, or has each its own proper part—the greater more, the smaller less? If this is so, then is one part of you greater, another less? Or are you wholly everywhere, while nothing altogether contains you?

FOUR

What are you then, my God—what, but the Lord God? *For who is Lord but the Lord? Or who is God save our God?* Most high, most excellent, most powerful, most almighty, most merciful, and most just; most hidden, yet most present; most beautiful, and most strong; stable, yet mysterious; unchangeable, yet changing all things; never new, never old; making all things new and *bringing age upon the proud, though they know it not*; ever working, yet ever at rest; still gathering, yet lacking nothing; sustaining, filling and protecting; creating, nourishing, and maturing; seeking, yet possessing all things. You love without passion; you are jealous without anxiety; you repent, yet have no sorrow; you are angry, yet serene; change your ways, yet your plans are unchanged; recover what you find, having never lost it; never in need, yet rejoicing in gain; never covetous, yet requiring interest. You receive over and above, that you may owe—yet who has anything that is not yours? You pay debts, owing nothing; remit debts, losing nothing. And what have I now said, my God, my life, my holy joy—what is this I have said? Or what do any say when they speak of you? Yet woe to those who keep silence, since those who say most are as the dumb!

BOOK XIII

From Inquiry to Praise

ONE

I call upon you, O my God, my Mercy, who made me and who did not forget me, though I forgot you. I call you into my soul, which you prepare for your reception by the longing you inspire in it. Do not forsake me now as I call on you who anticipated me before I called, and urged me with many kinds of repeated calls, that I should hear you from afar, be converted, and call upon you, who called me.

Lord, you blotted out all my evil desserts, not recompensing the work of my hands, by which I have acted rebelliously against you. And you have anticipated all my good desserts, so as to repay the work of your hands by which you made me, because before I came to be, you were, and I was not anything to which you might grant being. And yet, behold, I am—out of your goodness, anticipating all that you made me to be, and all out of which you made me. For you had no need of me, nor am I such a good one as to be helpful to you, my Lord and God; not in serving you, as though you were fatigued in working, or lest your power might be less if it lacked my assistance. Nor is my service to you like the cultivation of land, that you should go uncultivated if I did not cultivate you. But it is that I may serve and worship you to the end that I may have well-being from you, from whom I am one capable of well-being.

THREE

That you said in the beginning of the creation, *Let there be light, and there was light,* I understand to be the spiritual creation, because there was already a sort of life which you might illuminate. But just as it had no claim on you for a life that could be illuminated, so neither, when it already existed, had it any claim to be enlightened. For its formless condition could not be pleasing to you until it became light. And it became light not merely by existing, but by beholding the illuminating light and cleaving to it. It follows that it owes its living, and its living happily, to nothing but your grace, being turned by a change for the better toward that which cannot be changed for better or worse. That, you alone are, because you alone simply *are.* To you it is not one thing to live, another to live happily, because you, yourself, are your own blessedness.

EIGHT

Angels fell, the soul of man fell, and by this they have pointed out the abyss in that dark depth. That abyss was ready for the whole spiritual creation, if you had not said from the beginning, *Let there be light, and there was light*, and if every obedient intelligence of your heavenly City had not clung to you and rested in your Spirit—moving unchangeably over everything changeable. Otherwise, even the heaven of heavens would have been in itself a dark abyss; but now it is light in the Lord. For even in that miserable restlessness of the spirits who fell away, and when stripped of the garments of your light, discovered their own darkness, you sufficiently reveal how noble you made the rational creation, to which nothing less than you will suffice to produce a happy rest. It is not a rest even to itself. For you, O God, *shall lighten our darkness*. From you shall come our garments of light; and then *our darkness shall be as the noonday*.

Give yourself to me, O my God. Restore yourself to me. Behold I love you, and if it be too little, let me love you more strongly. I cannot measure my love, so that I may know how much love there is yet lacking in me before my life can run to your embrace and not be turned away, until it is hidden in the secret place of your Presence. This only I know: that woe is me except in you—not only outwardly, but also within myself. And all plenty that is not my God is poverty to me.

ST. CATHERINE OF SIENA

From *Little Talks with God*

"ARRIVING AT PURE AND GENEROUS LOVE"

From *Little Talks with God*, book III

A TREATISE OF PRAYER

Of the means that the soul takes to arrive at pure and generous love; here begins the Treatise of Prayer.

"When the soul has passed through the doctrine of Christ crucified, with true love of virtue and hatred of vice, and has arrived at the house of self-knowledge and entered into it, it remains, with its door barred, in watching and constant prayer, separated entirely from the consolations of the world. Why does it shut itself in this manner? It does so out of fear, knowing its own imperfections, and also from the desire of arriving at pure and generous love.

"And because the soul sees and knows well that in no other way can it arrive at pure love, with a lively faith it waits for my arrival, through the increase of grace in it.

"How is a lively faith to be recognized? By perseverance in virtue, and by the fact that the soul never turns back for anything, whatever it may be, nor rises from holy prayer for any reason except (note well) for obedience or charity's sake. For no other reason ought the soul to leave off prayer.

"For, during the time ordained for prayer, the devil is apt to arrive in the soul, causing much more conflict and trouble than when the soul is not occupied in prayer. This he does so that holy prayer may become tedious to the soul. He tempts the soul often with these words: 'This prayer avails you nothing, for you need attend to nothing except your vocal prayers.' He does this so that, becoming wearied and confused in mind, the soul may abandon the practice of prayer. For prayer is a weapon with which the soul can defend itself from every adversary, if it is grasped with the hand of love, by the arm of free choice in the light of the holy faith."

Here, concerning the sacrament of the body
of Christ, the complete doctrine is given; and
how the soul proceeds from vocal to mental
prayer, and a vision is related that this
devout servant of God once received.

"Know, dearest daughter, how, by humble, continual, and faithful prayer, with time and perseverance, the soul acquires every virtue. It should persevere and never abandon prayer, either through the illusion of the devil or its own fragility. That is, it should never abandon prayer either on account of any thought or movement coming from its own body, or on account of the words of any creature. The devil often places himself upon the tongues of creatures, causing them to chatter nonsensically, with the purpose of preventing the prayer of the soul. All of this the soul should pass by, by means of the virtue of perseverance.

"Oh, how sweet and pleasant to that soul and to me is holy prayer, made in the house of knowledge of self and of me. It opens the eye of the intellect to the light of faith and the affections to the abundance of my charity. And my charity was made visible to you through my visible, only-begotten Son, who showed it to you with his blood! This blood intoxicates the soul and clothes it with the fire of divine charity, giving it the food of the sacrament that is placed in the inn of the mystical body of the holy church. That is, the food of the body and blood of my Son, wholly God and wholly man, is administered to you by the hand of my vicar, who holds the key of the blood.

"This is the inn that I mentioned to you, the inn that stands on the bridge to provide food and comfort for the travelers and the pilgrims who pass by the way of the doctrine of my Truth, so they should not faint through weakness.

"This food strengthens little or much according to the desire of the recipient, whether he receives the food sacramentally or virtually. He receives the food sacramentally when he actually communicates with the blessed sacrament. He receives it virtually when he communicates, both by desire for communion and by contemplation of the blood of Christ crucified. It is as if he communicated sacramentally, with the affection of love. For love is to be tasted in the blood, which, as the soul sees, was shed through love. On seeing this the soul becomes intoxicated, and blazes with holy desire and satisfies itself, becoming full of love for me and for its neighbor.

"Where can this love be acquired? In the house of self-knowledge with holy prayer. There, imperfections are lost, even as Peter and the disciples, while they remained in watching and prayer, lost their imperfection and acquired perfection. By what means is this love acquired? By perseverance seasoned with the most holy faith.

"But do not think that the soul receives such ardor and nourishment from prayer if it prays only vocally, as do many souls whose prayers are words rather than love. Such as these give heed to nothing except to completing psalms and saying many Our Fathers. And once they have completed their appointed tale, they do not appear to think of anything further, but seem to place devout attention and love in mere vocal recitation. But the soul is not required to do this, for, in doing only this, it bears but little fruit, which pleases me but little.

"But if you asked me whether the soul should abandon vocal prayer, since it does not seem to everyone that they are called to mental prayer, I would reply 'No.' The soul should advance by degrees, and I know well that, just as the soul is at first imperfect and afterward perfect, so also is it with its prayer. It should nevertheless continue in vocal prayer, while it is yet imperfect, so as not to fall into idleness.

"But the soul should not say its vocal prayers without joining them to mental prayer. That is, while the soul is reciting vocal prayers, it should endeavor to elevate its mind in my love, with the consideration of its own defects and of the blood of my only-begotten Son. For in the Blood, it finds the breadth of my charity and the remission of its sins.

"And this the soul should do, so that self-knowledge and the consideration of its own defects should make it recognize my goodness in itself and continue its practices with true humility. I do not wish defects to be considered in particular, but in general, so that the mind may not be contaminated by the remembrance of particular and hideous sins.

"But I do not wish the soul to consider its sins, either in general or in particular, without also remembering the blood and the broadness of my mercy, for fear that otherwise it should be brought to confusion. And together with confusion would come the devil, who has caused it, under the banner of contrition and displeasure of sin. And so it would arrive at eternal damnation, not only because of its confusion, but also through the despair that would come to it, because it did not seize the arm of my mercy. This is one of the subtle devices with which the devil deludes my servants.

"In order to escape from the devil's deceit and to be pleasing to me, you must enlarge your hearts and affections in my boundless mercy, with true humility. You know that the pride of the devil cannot resist the humble mind, nor can any confusion of spirit be greater than the broadness of my good mercy, if the soul will only truly hope in my mercy.

"Once, if you remember rightly, when the devil wished to overthrow you by confusion, wishing to prove to you that your life had been deluded and that you had not followed my will, you did your duty, which my goodness (which is never withheld from one who will receive it) gave you strength to do. You rose, humbly trusting in my mercy, and said, 'I confess to my Creator that my life has indeed been passed in darkness. But I will hide myself in the wounds of Christ crucified, and bathe myself in his blood. And so shall my iniquities be consumed, and with desire will I rejoice in my creator.'

"You remember that then the devil fled. And, turning round to the opposite side, he endeavored to inflate you with pride, saying: 'You are perfect and pleasing to God, and there is no more need for you to afflict yourself or to lament your sins.' And once more I gave you the light to see your true path, namely, humiliation of yourself.

"And you answered the devil with these words: 'Wretch that I am, John the Baptist never sinned and was sanctified in his mother's womb. And I have committed so many sins, and have hardly begun to know them with grief and true contrition. For I see who God is, who is offended by me, and who I am, who offend him.'

"Then the devil, not being able to resist your humble hope in my goodness, said to you: 'Cursed that you are, for I can find no way to take you. If I put you down through confusion, you rise to heaven on the wings of mercy, and if I raise you on high, you humble yourself down to hell. And when I go into hell you persecute me, so that I will return to you no more, because you strike me with the stick of charity.'

"The soul, therefore, should season the knowledge of itself with the knowledge of my goodness, and then vocal prayer will be of use to the soul who prays it, and pleasing to me. And from the vocal imperfect prayer, practiced with perseverance, the soul will arrive at perfect mental prayer. But if it simply aims at completing its tale, and, preferring vocal prayer it abandons mental prayer, it will never arrive at it.

"Sometimes the soul will be so ignorant that, having resolved to say so many prayers vocally in order to complete its tale, it will abandon my visitation that it feels by conscience, rather than abandon what it had begun. For I visit its mind sometimes in one way, and sometimes in another. Sometimes I visit it in a flash of self-knowledge or of contrition for sin, sometimes in the broadness of my charity. Sometimes I place before its mind, in various ways, according to my pleasure and the desire of the soul, the presence of my Truth.

"The soul should not abandon my visitation, for, in doing so, it yields to a deception of the devil. The moment it feels its mind disposed by my visitation in the many ways I have told you, it should abandon vocal prayer. Then, once my visitation has passed, if there is time it can resume the vocal prayers it resolved to say. But if it does not have time to complete them, it ought not on that account to be troubled or suffer annoyance and confusion of mind.

"Of course I am not referring to the Divine Office, which clerics and religious are bound and obliged to say under penalty of offending me, for, they must, until death, say their office. But if they, at the hour appointed for saying it, should feel their minds drawn and raised by desire, they should arrange so as to say the office before or after my visitation. Thus they will assure that the debt of rendering the office is not omitted.

"But in any other case, vocal prayer should be abandoned immediately for my visitation. Vocal prayer, made in the way that I have told you, will enable the soul to arrive at perfection. Therefore the soul should not abandon it, but use it in the way that I have told you.

"And so, with practice in perseverance, the soul will in truth taste prayer, and the food of the blood of my only-begotten Son. Therefore I told you that some communicate virtually with the body and blood of Christ, although not sacramentally. That is, they communicate in the affection of charity, which they taste by means of holy prayer. They communicate little or much, according to the affection with which they pray. Those who proceed with little prudence and without method, taste little, and those who proceed with much, taste much.

"For the more the soul tries to loosen its affection from itself and fasten it in me with the light of the intellect, the more it knows. And the more the soul knows, the more it loves. And, loving much, it tastes much.

"You see then, that perfect prayer is not arrived at through many words, but through affection of desire, when the soul raises itself to me, knowing itself and my mercy, seasoned the one with the other. Thus the soul will practice mental and vocal prayer together, for, even as the active and contemplative life are one, so are they.

"Now, vocal or mental prayer can be understood in many different ways. For I have told you that a holy desire is a continual prayer, in the sense that a good and holy will disposes itself with desire to the occasion actually appointed for prayer, in addition to the continual prayer of holy desire. Therefore vocal prayer will be made at the appointed time by the soul who remains firm in a habitual holy will. And sometimes vocal prayer will be continued beyond the appointed time. The length of time will vary according as charity commands for the salvation of one's neighbor, if the soul sees him in need. And it will vary according to the soul's own needs, which depend on the state in which I have placed it.

"Each person, according to his condition, ought to exert himself for the salvation of souls. For this exercise lies at the root of a holy will. Whatever he may contribute, by words or deeds, toward the salvation of his neighbor, is virtually a prayer. But keep in mind that it does not replace a prayer that one should make oneself at the appointed season.

"As my glorious standard-bearer Paul said, 'He who ceases not to work ceases not to pray.' It was for this reason that I told you that prayer is made in many ways. That is, actual prayer may be united with mental prayer if it is made with the affection of charity, for charity is itself continual prayer.

"I have now told you how mental prayer is reached by exercise and perseverance, and by leaving off vocal prayer in favor of mental, when I visit the soul. I have also spoken to you of common prayer, that is, of vocal prayer in general, made outside of ordained times. And I have spoken to you of the prayers of good-will, and how every exercise, whether performed in oneself or in one's neighbor, with good-will, is prayer. The enclosed soul should therefore spur itself on with prayer. And when it has arrived at friendly and filial love, it does so. Unless the soul keeps to this path, it will always remain tepid and imperfect, and will love me and its neighbor only in proportion to the pleasure it finds in my service."

Of the method by which the soul separates
itself from imperfect love and attains to
perfect love, friendly and filial.

"Until now I have shown you in many ways how the soul raises itself from imperfection and attains to perfection. And this it does after it has attained to friendly and filial love. I tell you that it arrives at perfect love by means of perseverance, barring itself into the house of self-knowledge.

"Now, knowledge of self must be seasoned with knowledge of me, lest it bring the soul to confusion. For self-knowledge would cause the soul to hate its own sensitive pleasure and the delight of its own consolations. But from this hatred, founded in humility, it will draw patience. With patience it will become strong against the attacks of the devil, against the persecutions of man, and toward me, when, for its good, I withdraw delight from its mind.

"And if the soul's sensuality, through malevolence, should lift its head against reason, the judgment of conscience will rise against it. With hatred of it, the judgment of conscience will hold out reason against it, not allowing such evil emotions to get by it.

"However, sometimes the soul who lives in holy hatred corrects and rebukes itself, not only for the things that are against reason, but also for things that in reality come from me. This is what my sweet servant St. Gregory meant when he said that a holy and pure conscience makes sin where there was no sin. That is, through purity of conscience the soul sees sin where there is no sin.

"Now the soul who wishes to rise above imperfection should await my providence in the house of self-knowledge, with the light of faith, as did the disciples. For the disciples remained in the house in perseverance, in watching, and in humble and continual prayer, awaiting the coming of the Holy Spirit. The soul should remain fasting and watching, with the eye of its intellect fastened on the doctrine of my truth. And it will become humble because it will know itself in humble and continual prayer and in holy and true desire."

*Of the signs by which the soul knows it
has arrived at perfect love.*

"It now remains to tell you how it can be seen that souls have arrived at perfect love: by the same sign that was given to the holy disciples after they received the Holy Spirit. At that time they came forth from the house and fearlessly announced the doctrine of my Word, my only-begotten Son, not fearing pain, but rather glorying in it. They did not mind going before the tyrants of the world to announce the truth to them for the glory and praise of my name.

"So the soul who has awaited me in self-knowledge receives me, on my return to it, with the fire of charity. In charity, while still remaining in the house with perseverance, it conceives the virtues by affection of love and participates in my power.

"With my power and these virtues, this soul overrules and conquers its own sensitive passions, and through charity it participates in the wisdom of my Son. In wisdom it sees and knows my truth, with the eye of its intellect. And it knows the deceptions of spiritual self-love, that is, the imperfect love of its own consolations. It also knows the malice and deceit of the devil, which he practices on those souls who are bound by that imperfect love.

"Therefore this soul arises with hatred of that imperfection and with love of perfection. And, through this love, which is of the Holy Spirit, it participates in his will, fortifying itself to be willing to suffer pain. Then, coming out of the house through my name, it brings forth the virtues on its neighbor.

"Not that by 'coming out to bring forth the virtues,' I mean that the soul leaves the house of self-knowledge. Rather, in the time of its neighbor's need it loses the fear of being deprived of its own consolations, and so it sets out to give birth to those virtues that it has conceived through affection of love.

"The souls who have come forth in this manner have reached the fourth state, which is that of perfect union with me. The two last-mentioned states are united, that is, the one cannot exist without the other. For there cannot be love of me without love of one's neighbor, nor love of the neighbor without love of me."

*How worldly people render glory and praise
to God, whether they want to or not.*

A nd so perfect is the soul's vision that it sees the glory and praise of my name, not so much in the angelic nature as in the human. For whether worldly people want to or not, they render glory and praise to my name. Not that they do so in the way they should, loving me above everything, but my mercy shines in them, in the abundance of my charity. I give them time, and I do not order the earth to open and swallow them up on account of their sins. I even wait for them, and command the earth to give them of its fruits, the sun to give them light and warmth, and the sky to move above them. And in all things created and made for them, I use my charity and mercy, withdrawing neither on account of their sins.

"I even give equally to the sinner and to the righteous man, and often more to the sinner than to the righteous man. For the righteous man is able to endure privation, and I take from him the goods of the world so that he may the more abundantly enjoy the goods of heaven. So in worldly men my mercy and charity shine, and they render praise and glory to my name even when they persecute my servants. For they prove in my servants the virtues of patience and charity, causing them to suffer humbly and to offer me their persecutions and injuries, thus turning them into my praise and glory.

"So that, whether they want to or not, worldly people render praise and glory to my name, when they intend to do me infamy and wrong."

How even the devils render glory and praise to God.

"Sinners, such as those of whom I have just spoken, are placed in this life in order to augment the virtues in my servants. In the same way the devils are in hell to serve as my instruments of justice toward the damned. They also serve to augment my glory in my creatures, who are wayfarers and pilgrims on their journey to reach me, their end.

"The devils augment the virtues in my creatures in various ways, exercising them with many temptations and vexations and causing them to injure one another and to take one another's property. This they do, not for the motive of making them receive injury or be deprived of their property, but only to deprive them of charity. But in thinking to deprive my servants, the sinners and devils strengthen them, proving in them the virtues of patience, fortitude, and perseverance. In this way, devils render praise and glory to my name, and my truth is fulfilled in them.

"Now, my truth created the devils for the praise and glory of me, the eternal Father, and so that they might participate in my beauty. But, rebelling against me in their pride, they fell and lost their vision of me. Therefore they did not render to me glory through the affection of love.

"So I, eternal Truth, have placed the devils as instruments to exercise my servants in virtue in this life and as judicial officers to those who go, for their sins, to the pains of Purgatory. So you see that my truth is fulfilled in them, that is, in that they render me glory, not as citizens of life eternal, of which they are deprived by their sins, but as my officers. As such they manifest justice upon the damned, and upon those in Purgatory."

*How the soul, after it has passed through this
life, sees fully the praise and glory of my name
in everything, and though in it the pain of
desire is ended, the desire itself is not.*

Thus in all things created—in all rational creatures and in all devils—is seen the glory and praise of my name. Who can see it? The soul who has left the body and has reached me, its end, sees it clearly, and, in seeing, knows the truth. Seeing me, the eternal Father, it loves. And loving, it is satisfied. Satisfied, it knows the truth, and its will is stayed in my will, bound and made stable. Therefore in nothing can it suffer pain, because it has what it desired to have before it saw me, namely, the glory and praise of my name.

"So now, in truth, this soul sees my glory completely in my saints, in the blessed spirits, and in all creatures and things, even in the devils. And although it also sees the injury done to me, which before caused it sorrow, the injury no longer now can give it pain, but only compassion. And this is because it loves without pain, and prays to me continually, with affection of love, that I will have mercy on the world.

"Pain in this soul is ended, but not love, just as the tortured desire which my Word, the Son, had borne from the beginning when I sent him into the world, ended on the cross in his painful death—but not his love. For if the love that I showed you by means of my Son had terminated and ended then, you would not exist, because by love you are made. And if my love been drawn back, you could not exist. My love created you, and my love possesses you, because I am one with my Truth, and he, the Word incarnate, is one with me.

"You see then, that the saints and every soul in eternal life desire the salvation of souls without pain, because pain ended in their death, but not so the affection of love.

"Thus, as if intoxicated with the blood of the immaculate Lamb and clothed in the love of their neighbor, they pass through the narrow gate. There, bathed in the blood of Christ crucified, they find themselves in me, the Sea of Peace. Raised from imperfection, far from satiety, they have arrived at perfection, and are satisfied by every good."

How the soul who finds itself in the unitive state
desires infinitely to unite itself to God.

When I depart from the soul so that the body may return a little to its bodily sentiment, the soul, on account of the union that it had made with me, is impatient in its life. It becomes tired of being deprived of union with me and the conversation of the immortals who render glory to me. And it grows weary of finding itself amid the conversation of mortals, and of seeing them so miserably offending me.

"This vision of offenses against me is the torture that such souls always have. And that torture, along with the desire to see me, renders their life intolerable to them. Nevertheless, as their will is not their own, but becomes one with mine, they cannot desire other than what I desire. Though they desire to come and be with me, they are content to remain with their pain, if I desire them to remain, for the greater praise and glory of my name and the salvation of souls. So in nothing are these souls in discord with my will, but they run their course with ecstatic desire, clothed in Christ crucified, and keeping by the bridge of his doctrine, glorying in his shame and pains.

"As much as these souls appear to be suffering, they are rejoicing, because enduring many tribulations is to them a relief in the desire that they have for death. For often their desire and their will to suffer pain mitigates the pain caused them by their desire to leave the body.

"These who are in the third state not only endure with patience, but they glory, through my name, in bearing much tribulation. In bearing tribulation they find pleasure, and when I permit to them many tribulations they rejoice, seeing themselves clothed with the suffering and shame of Christ crucified.

"Therefore if it were possible for these souls to have virtue without toil, they would not want it. They would rather delight in the Cross, with Christ, acquiring virtue with pain, than to obtain eternal life in any other way. Why? Because they are inflamed and steeped in the Blood, where they find the blaze of my charity. For my charity is a fire proceeding from me, ravishing their heart and mind and making their sacrifices acceptable.

"Thus, when the affection behind the intellect is nourished and united with me, the eye of the intellect is lifted up and gazes into my deity. This is a sight that I grant to the soul infused with grace who, in truth, loves and serves me."

How those who have arrived at the unitive
state have the eye of their intellect illuminated
by supernatural light, infused by grace. And
how it is better to go for counsel, for the salvation
of the soul, to a humble and holy conscience
than to a proud man of letters.

"With this light that is given to the eye of the intellect, Thomas Aquinas saw me, and for that reason he acquired the light of much knowledge. Augustine, Jerome, the teachers of the church, and my saints were illuminated by my truth to know and understand my truth in the midst of darkness.

"By my truth I mean the Holy Scripture, which seemed dark because it was not understood. And this was not through any defect of the Scriptures, but of those who heard them and did not understand them. Therefore I sent the light of the Holy Scripture to illuminate men's blind and coarse understanding, and to lift up the eye of their intellect to know the truth. And I, Fire, Acceptor of sacrifices, ravishing away from them their darkness, give them light.

"This was not a natural light, but a supernatural one, so that, though in darkness, men might know the truth. So you see that the eye of the intellect has received supernatural light, infused by grace, by which the teachers and saints knew light in darkness. And of darkness they made light.

"The intellect existed before the Scriptures were formed. Therefore from the intellect came knowledge, because in seeing, they discerned. It was in this way that the holy prophets and fathers understood, they who prophesied of the coming and death of my Son. And it was in this way that the apostles understood, after the coming of the Holy Spirit, who gave them that supernatural light. The evangelists, doctors, professors, virgins, and martyrs were all likewise illuminated by that perfect light. And everyone has had the illumination of this light as he needed it for his salvation or that of others, or for the exposition of the Scriptures.

"The teachers of holy knowledge had it as they expounded on the doctrine of my truth, the preaching of the apostles, and the Gospels of the evangelists. The martyrs had it, declaring in their blood the most holy faith, the fruit and the treasure of the blood of the Lamb. The virgins had it in the affection of charity and purity.

"To the obedient ones is declared, by this light, the obedience of the Word, showing them the perfection of obedience, which shines in my Truth. And my Truth, for the obedience that I imposed upon him, ran to the public disgrace of the cross.

"This light is to be seen in the Old and New Testaments. In the Old, by it the prophecies of the holy prophets were seen by the eye of the intellect, and known. In the New Testament of the evangelical life, how is the gospel declared to the faithful? By this same light.

"And because the New Testament proceeded from the same light, the new law did not break the old law. Rather, the two laws are bound together. The imperfection of the old law, founded in fear alone, was taken from it by the coming of the Word of my only-begotten Son with the law of love. He completed the old law by giving it love, and replaced the fear of penalty by holy fear. And, to show that he was not a breaker of laws my Truth said to the disciples: 'I came not to dissolve the law, but to fulfill it.'

"It is almost as if my Truth would say to them—The law is now imperfect, but with my blood I will make it perfect, and I will fill it up with what it lacks. I will take away the fear of penalty and found it on love and holy fear. How was this declared to be the truth? By this same supernatural light, which was and is given by grace to all.

"Now, who will receive this light? Every light that comes from holy Scripture comes and came from this supernatural light. Ignorant and proud men of science were blind notwithstanding this light, because their pride and the cloud of self-love covered up and put out the light. For that reason they understood the holy Scripture literally rather than with understanding, and tasted only the letter of it, still desiring many other books.

"Such men do not get to the heart of the Scripture, because they have deprived themselves of the light with which the Scripture is found and expounded. They are annoyed and they murmur, because they find much in Scripture that appears to them gross and idiotic.

"Nevertheless, such men appear to be much enlightened in their knowledge of Scripture, as if they had studied it for long. This is not remarkable, because of course they have the natural light from which science proceeds. But because they have lost the supernatural light, infused by grace, they neither see nor know my goodness, nor the grace of my servants.

"Therefore, I say to you, it is much better to go for counsel for the salvation of the soul, to a person of holy and upright conscience, than to a proud man of letters who has learned much knowledge. Such a one can offer only what he has himself, and, because of his darkness, it may appear to you that, from what he says, the Scriptures offer darkness. You will find the opposite with my servants, because they offer the light that is in them, with hunger and desire for the soul's salvation.

"This I have told you, my sweetest daughter, that you might know the perfection of this union-producing state, when the eye of the intellect is ravished by the fire of my charity, in which it receives the supernatural light. With this light the souls in the state of union love me, because love follows the intellect, and the more it knows the more it can love. So the one feeds the other, and, with this light, they both arrive at the eternal vision of me, in which vision they see and taste me, in truth.

"At this point the soul becomes separated from the body, as I told you when I spoke to you of the blissfulness that the soul receives in me. This state is most excellent, for the soul, being yet in the mortal body, tastes bliss with the immortals. Often it arrives at so great a union that it scarcely knows whether it is in the body or out of it. It tastes the pledge of eternal life, both because it is united with me, and because its will is dead in Christ. By that death its union is made with me, and indeed in no other way can it perfectly do so. Souls in this state of union taste life eternal. And they are divested of the hell of their own will, which gives to man the pledge of damnation if he yields to it."

How this devout servant of God seeks knowledge from
God concerning the state and fruit of tears.

T hen this servant of God, yearning with very great desire,
rose as if intoxicated both by the union that she had had
with God, and by what she had heard and tasted of the supreme
and sweet truth. And she yearned with grief over the ignorance of
creatures in that they did not know their benefactor, or the affection
of the love of God. Nevertheless she had joy from the hope of the
promise that the Truth of God had made to her. For he had taught
the way she was to direct her will (and the other servants of God as
well as herself) so that he might show mercy to the world.

Lifting up the eye of her intellect upon the sweet Truth, to
whom she remained united, this servant wished to know something of the states of the soul of which God had spoken to
her. Seeing that the soul passes through these states with tears,
she wished to learn from the Truth about the different kinds
of tears. She desired to know how they came to be, and from
where they proceeded, and the fruit that resulted from weeping. And she wished to know from the sweet, supreme, and
first Truth himself as to the manner of being of tears and the
reason for them.

Inasmuch as the truth cannot be learned from any other than
the Truth himself, and nothing can be learned in the Truth but
what is seen by the eye of the intellect, she made her request of the
Truth. For it is necessary for one who is lifted with desire to learn
the truth with the light of faith. She had not forgotten the teaching that the Truth, that is, God, had given her, that in no other
way could she learn about the different states and fruits of tears.

Therefore this servant rose out of herself, exceeding every limit of her nature with the greatness of her desire. And with the light of a lively faith, she opened the eye of her intellect upon the eternal Truth, in whom she saw and knew the truth, in the matter of her request. For God himself manifested it to her, and, condescending in his kindness to her burning desire, he fulfilled her petition.

How there are five kinds of tears.

Then said the supreme and sweet Truth of God, "Beloved and dearest daughter, you beg knowledge of the reasons and fruits of tears, and I have not despised your desire. Open wide the eye of your intellect, and I will show you the various kinds of tears.

"The first are the tears of the wicked men of the world. These are the tears of damnation.

"The second are the imperfect tears caused by fear. These belong to those who abandon sin from fear of punishment and weep out of fear.

"The third are the tears of those who, having abandoned sin, are beginning to serve and taste me, and weep for very sweetness. But since their love is imperfect, so also is their weeping.

"The fourth are the tears of those who have arrived at the perfect love of their neighbor, loving me without any regard whatsoever for themselves. These weep, and their weeping is perfect. The fifth are joined to the fourth and are tears of sweetness shed with great peace.

"I will explain all these to you. And I will tell you also of the tears of fire that involve no bodily tears of the eyes, but satisfy those who often would desire to weep and cannot.

"And I want you to know that all these various graces may exist in one soul, who, rising from fear and imperfect love, reaches perfect love in the union-producing state. Now I will begin to tell you about these tears."

Of the differences among these tears, arising from the explanation of the aforesaid state of the soul.

"I wish you to know that every tear proceeds from the heart, for there is no member of the body that will satisfy the heart so much as the eye. If the heart is in pain, the eye manifests it. And if the pain is sensual the eye drops hearty tears that engender death. For, proceeding from the heart, they are caused by a disordinate love distinct from the love of me. Such love, being disordinate and an offense to me, receives the reward of mortal pain and tears. And these form that first class, who shed the tears of death.

"Now, begin to consider the tears that give the beginning of life, that is, the tears of those who, knowing their guilt, set to weeping for fear of the penalty they have incurred. These are both hearty and sensual tears, because the soul, not having yet arrived at perfect hatred of its guilt on account of the offense done to me, abandons its guilt with grief in its heart for the penalty that follows the sin committed. So the eye weeps in order to satisfy the grief of the heart.

"But the soul, exercising itself in virtue, begins to lose its fear, knowing that fear alone is not sufficient to give it eternal life. And so it proceeds, with love, to know itself and my goodness in it, and begins to take hope in my mercy, in which its heart feels joy. Sorrow for its grief, mingled with the joy of its hope in my mercy, causes its eye to weep. And these tears issue from the very fountain of its heart.

"But, inasmuch as this soul has not yet arrived at great perfection, it often drops sensual tears. If you ask me why, I reply: Because the root of self-love is not sensual love, for that has already been removed. Rather, it is a spiritual love with which the soul desires spiritual consolations or loves some creature spiritually.

"Therefore, when such a soul is deprived of the thing it loves, that is, internal or external consolation (the internal being the consolation received from me, the external being that which it had from the creature), and when temptations and persecutions come on it, its heart is full of grief. And, as soon as its eye feels the grief and suffering of the heart, it begins to weep with a tender and compassionate sorrow, pitying itself with the spiritual compassion of self-love. For its self-will is not yet crushed and destroyed in everything, and in this way it sheds sensual tears—tears, that is, of spiritual passion.

"But, growing and exercising itself in the light of self-knowledge, the soul conceives displeasure at itself and finally perfect self-hatred. From this it draws true knowledge of my goodness with the fire of love. And then it begins to unite itself to me, and to conform its will to mine and so to feel joy and compassion. It feels joy in itself through the affection of love, and it feels compassion for its neighbor.

"Immediately its eye, wishing to satisfy the heart, cries with hearty love for me and for its neighbor, grieving solely for offenses done to me and for its neighbor's loss, and for any penalty or loss due to itself. It no longer thinks of itself, but only of rendering glory and praise to my name.

"Then, in an ecstasy of desire, it joyfully takes the food prepared for it on the table of the holy cross. In so doing, it conforms itself to the humble, patient, and immaculate Lamb, my only-begotten Son, of whom I made a bridge.

"Now this soul has traveled by that bridge, and has followed the doctrine of my Truth. It has endured with true and sweet patience every pain and trouble that I have permitted to be inflicted upon it for its salvation, manfully receiving them all. It has not chosen its afflictions according to its own tastes, but has accepted them according to mine. And not only has this soul endured its trials with patience, but it has also sustained them with joy. Therefore the soul counts it glory to be persecuted for my name's sake in whatever it may have to suffer.

"Then the soul rests in me, the Sea of Peace, and has such delight and tranquillity of mind that no tongue can tell it. It has crossed the river by means of the eternal Word, that is, by the doctrine of my only-begotten Son, and, has fixed the eye of its intellect on Me, the Sweet Supreme Truth. Having seen the Truth, the soul knows it; and knowing the Truth, the soul loves it. Drawing its affection after its intellect, it tastes my eternal deity, and it knows and sees the divine nature united to your humanity.

"Then the soul rests in me, the Sea of Peace, and its heart is united to me in love. When it in such a manner feels me, the eternal deity, its eyes shed tears of sweetness, tears indeed of milk, nourishing the soul in true patience. These tears are a sweet-smelling ointment, shedding odors of great sweetness.

"Oh, best beloved daughter, how glorious is the soul who has indeed been able to pass from the stormy ocean to me, the Sea of Peace, and in that sea, which is myself, the supreme and eternal deity, has been able to fill the pitcher of its heart. And its eye, the conduit of its heart, endeavors to satisfy its heart-pangs, and so it sheds tears. This is the last stage in which the soul is blessed and sorrowful.

"Blessed is the soul through the union that it feels itself to have with me, tasting the divine love. Sorrowful is the soul through the offenses that it sees done to my goodness and greatness, for in its self-knowledge it has seen and tasted the bitterness of such offenses. By this self-knowledge, together with its knowledge of me, it has arrived at the final stage.

"Yet sorrow is no impediment to the state of union that produces tears of great sweetness through self-knowledge, gained in love of one's neighbor. For in this exercise the soul discovers the plaint of my divine mercy, and grief at the offenses caused to its neighbor. And it weeps with those who weep, and rejoices with those who rejoice—that is, who live in my love. Over these the soul rejoices, seeing glory and praise rendered me by my servants.

"The third kind of grief does not prevent the fourth, that is, the final grief belonging to the unitive state. They give savor to each other, for, if this last grief (in which the soul finds such union with me), had not developed from the grief belonging to the third state of neighborly love, it would not be perfect. Therefore it is necessary that the one should flavor the other, or else the soul would come to a state of presumption, induced by the subtle breeze of love of its own reputation, and would fall at once, vomited from the heights to the depths. Therefore it is necessary to bear with others and to continually practice love of one's neighbor, together with true knowledge of oneself.

"In this way the soul will feel the fire of my love in itself, because love of its neighbor is developed out of love of me. That is, it is developed out of the learning that the soul obtained by knowing itself and my goodness in it. Therefore, when the soul sees itself inexpressibly loved by me, it loves every rational creature with the exact same love with which it sees itself loved.

"And, for this reason, the soul who knows me immediately expands to the love of its neighbor, because it sees that I love that neighbor indescribably. And so it loves still more the object that it sees me to have loved. It further knows that it can be of no use to me and can in no way repay me that pure love with which it feels that I love it. Therefore it endeavors to repay that love through the medium I have given it, namely, its neighbor. For one's neighbor is the medium through which you can all serve me. You can perform all virtues by means of your neighbor. Therefore you should love your neighbor with the same pure love with which I have loved you. You cannot return that pure love directly to me, because I have loved you without being myself loved, and without any consideration of myself whatsoever.

"I loved you without being loved by you—before you existed. It was, indeed, love that moved me to create you in my own image and likeness. This love you cannot repay to me, but you can pay it to my rational creature. And this you can do by loving your neighbor without his loving you and without consideration of your own advantage, whether spiritual or temporal. You can love him solely for the praise and glory of my name, because I have loved him. In this way you will fulfill the commandment of the law, to love me above everything, and your neighbor as yourself.

"It is true indeed is it that this height cannot be reached without passing through the second stage. Nor can this height be preserved when it has been reached if the soul abandons the affection from which it has been developed, the affection to which the second class of tears belongs. It is therefore impossible to fulfill the law given by me, the eternal God, without fulfilling the law of loving your neighbor. For these two laws were given you by my Truth, Christ crucified. When united, these two states nourish your soul in virtue, making it to grow in the perfection of virtue and in the state of union.

"Not that the other state is changed because this further state has been reached. No, this further state only increases the riches of grace in new and various gifts and admirable elevations of the mind. It does so in the knowledge of the truth, which, though it is mortal, appears immortal because the soul's perception of its own sensuality is mortified, and its will is dead through the union that it has attained with me.

"Oh, how sweet is the taste of this union to the soul, for, in tasting it, it sees my secrets! Therefore it often receives the spirit of prophecy, knowing the things of the future. This is the effect of my goodness, but the humble soul should despise such things, not indeed insofar as they are given it by my love, but insofar as it desires them by reason of its appetite for consolation. It should consider itself unworthy of peace and quiet of mind, in order to nourish virtue within it.

"In such a case it must not remain in the second stage, but must return to the valley of self-knowledge. I give it this light, my grace permitting, so that it may ever grow in virtue. For the soul is never so perfect in this life that it cannot attain to a higher perfection of love.

"My only-begotten Son, your captain, was the only one who could not increase in perfection, because he was one with me, and I with him. Therefore his soul was blessed through union with the divine nature.

"But you, his pilgrim-members, must be ever ready to grow in greater perfection. This is not to say that you will move to another stage, for as I have said, you have now reached the last one. But you are to grow to that further grade of perfection in the last stage, which may please you by means of my grace."

How the four stages of the soul,
to which the five states of tears belong,
produce tears of infinite value; and how God wishes
to be served as the Infinite, and not as anything finite.

"These five states are like five principal canals filled with abundant tears of infinite value, all of which give life if they are disciplined in virtue. You ask how their value can be infinite. I do not say that in this life your tears can become infinite, but I call them infinite, on account of the infinite desire of your soul from which they proceed.

"I have already told you how tears come from the heart, and how the heart distributes them to the eye, having gathered them in its own fiery desire. When green wood is on the fire, the moisture it contains groans on account of the heat, because the wood is green. So does the heart, made green again by the renewal of grace drawn into the midst of its self-love. And grace dries up the soul, so that fiery desire and tears are united.

"Inasmuch as desire is never ended, it is never satisfied in this life, but the more the soul loves, the less it seems to itself to love. Thus is holy desire, which is founded in love and exercised, and with this desire the eye weeps. But when the soul is separated from the body and has reached me, its end, it does not on that account abandon desire, so as to no longer yearn for me or love its neighbor. For love has entered into it like a woman bearing the fruits of all other virtues.

"It is true that suffering is over and ended, for the soul who desires me possesses me in very truth, without any fear of ever losing what it has so long desired. But, in this way, hunger continues: Those who are hungry are satisfied, and as soon as they are satisfied, they hunger again. In this way their satisfaction is without disgust, and their hunger is without suffering, for, in me, no perfection is lacking.

"Thus your desire is infinite, or otherwise it would be worth nothing. Nor would any virtue of yours have any life if you served me with anything finite. For I, who am the infinite God, wish you to serve me with infinite service. And the only infinite thing you possess is the affection and desire of your souls. In this sense there are tears of infinite value, and this is true because of the infinite desire that is united to the tears.

"When the soul leaves the body the tears remain behind, but the affection of love has drawn to itself the fruit of the tears, and has consumed it, just as happens to the water in your furnace: The water has not really been taken out of the furnace, but the heat of the fire has consumed it and drawn it into itself.

"Thus the soul, having arrived at tasting the fire of my divine charity, and having passed from this life in a state of love toward me and its neighbor, having further possessed the uniting love that caused its tears to fall, does not cease to offer me its blessed desires. It is tearful indeed, though without pain or physical weeping. For physical tears have evaporated in the furnace and have become tears of fire of the Holy Spirit.

"You see then how tears are infinite. For as regards the tears shed in this life only, no tongue can tell what different sorrows may cause them. I have now told you the difference among four of these states of tears."

Of the fruit of worldly men's tears.

"It remains for me to tell you of the fruit produced by tears shed with desire and received into the soul. But first I will speak to you of that first class of men whom I mentioned at the beginning of this discourse. I am referring to those who live miserably in the world, making a god of created things and of their own sensuality, from which comes damage to their body and soul. I said to you that every tear proceeds from the heart. And this is the truth, for the heart grieves in proportion to the love it feels. So worldly persons weep when their heart feels pain, that is, when they are deprived of something they love.

"But their complainings are many and diverse. Do you know how many? There are as many as there are different loves. And inasmuch as the root of self-love is corrupt, everything that grows from it is corrupt also. Self-love is a tree on which grows nothing but fruits of death, putrid flowers, stained leaves, branches bowed down and struck by various winds. This is the tree of the soul.

"For you are all trees of love, and without love you cannot live, for you have been made by me for love. The soul who lives virtuously places the root of its tree in the valley of true humility. But those who live miserably are planted on the mountain of pride.

"From this it follows that since the root of the tree is badly planted, the tree can bear no fruits of life, but only of death. Their fruits are their actions, which are all poisoned by many kinds of sin. And if they should produce some good fruit among their actions, even that good fruit will be spoiled by the foulness of its root. For no good action done by a soul in mortal sin is of value for eternal life, seeing that it is not done in grace.

"However, such a soul must not abandon its good works on this account. For every good deed is rewarded, and every evil deed punished. A good action performed outside of a state of grace is not sufficient to merit eternal life. But my justice, my divine goodness, grants an incomplete reward, as imperfect as the action that obtains it. Often such a person is rewarded in temporal matters. Sometimes I give that soul more time in which to repent. And sometimes I grant to that soul the life of grace by means of my servants who are pleasing and acceptable to me.

"I acted in this way with my glorious apostle Paul, who abandoned his refusal to believe, and the persecutions he directed against the Christians, upon hearing the prayer of St. Stephen. Therefore, in whatever state a person may be, he should never stop doing good.

"I said to you that the flowers of this tree are putrid, and so in truth they are. Its flowers are the stinking thoughts of the heart, displeasing to me and full of hatred and unkindness toward its neighbor. So if a person is a thief, he robs me of honor and takes it himself.

"This flower stinks less than that of false judgment, which is of two kinds. The first kind of false judgment is in regards to me. Those who are guilty of this false judgment judge my secret judgments and gauge falsely all my mysteries. That is, they judge that which I did in love to have been done in hatred; that which I did in truth to have been done in falsehood; that which I give them for life, to have been given them for death. They condemn and judge everything according to their weak intellect. For they have blinded the eye of their intellect with sensual self-love, and hidden the pupil of the most holy faith, which they will not allow to see or know the truth.

"The second kind of false judgment is directed against one's neighbor. From this judgment often come many evils, because the wretched person wishes to set himself up as the judge of the affections and heart of other rational creatures, when he does not yet know himself. And, from an action that he may see, or from a word he may hear, he will judge the affection of the heart.

"My servants always judge well, because they are founded on me, the supreme good. But such as these always judge badly, for they are founded on evil. Such critics as these cause hatreds, murders, and unhappinesses of all kinds to their neighbors. And they remove themselves far away from the love of my servants' virtue.

"Truly these fruits follow the leaves, which are the words that issue from their mouth insulting me and the blood of my only-begotten Son, and showing hatred to their neighbors. And they think of nothing else but cursing and condemning my works, and blaspheming and saying evil of every rational creature, as their judgment may suggest to them.

"These unfortunate creatures do not remember that the tongue is made only to give honor to me, and to confess sins, and to be used in love of virtue, and for the salvation of one's neighbor. These are the stained leaves of that most miserable fault, because the heart from which they proceed is not clean, but is all spotted with duplicity and misery.

"Apart from the spiritual privation of grace to the soul, how much danger of temporal loss may occur! For you have heard and seen how, through words alone, have come revolutions of states, destructions of cities, and many homicides and other evils. For a word entered the heart of the listener and passed through a space not large enough for a knife.

"This tree has seven branches drooping to the earth, on which grow the flowers and leaves. These branches are the seven mortal sins, which are full of many and diverse wickednesses. And these wickednesses are contained in the roots and trunk of self-love and of pride, which first made both branches and flowers of many thoughts, leaves of words, and fruits of wicked deeds.

"The seven branches stand drooping to the earth, because the branches of mortal sin can turn no other way than to the earth, the fragile, disordinate substance of the world. Do not marvel: they can turn no way but that in which they can be fed by the earth. For their hunger is insatiable, and the earth is unable to satisfy them.

"It is conformable to their state that they should always be unquiet, longing and desiring the thing with which they are filled to excess. This is why such excess cannot content them.

For they (who are infinite in their being) are always desiring something finite. Yet their being will never end, though their life to grace ends when they commit mortal sin.

"Man is placed above all creatures, and not beneath them, and he cannot be satisfied or content except in something greater than himself. Greater than himself there is nothing but myself, the eternal God. Therefore I alone can satisfy him. And, because he is deprived of this satisfaction by his guilt, he remains in continual torment and pain. Weeping follows pain, and when he begins to weep the wind strikes the tree of self-love, which he has made the principle of all his being."

How this devout soul, thanking God for his explanation
of the above-mentioned states of tears, makes three petitions.

Then this servant of God, eager with the greatness of her desire, through the sweetness of the explanation and satisfaction that she had received from the Truth, concerning the state of tears, said as one full of love—"Thanks, thanks be to you, supreme and eternal Father, satisfier of holy desires, and lover of our salvation, who, through your love, gave us Love himself. And you did this in the time of our warfare with you, in the person of your only-begotten Son.

"By this abyss of your fiery love, I beg of you grace and mercy to come to you truly in the light, and not to flee far in darkness away from your doctrine. You have clearly demonstrated to me the truth of your doctrine, so that, by its light, I may perceive two other points. Concerning these, I fear that they are, or may become, stumbling-blocks to me.

"I beg, eternal Father, that, before I leave the subject of these states of tears, you would explain these points also to me. The first is—when a person who desires to serve you comes to me or to some other servant of yours to ask for counsel, how should I teach him?

"I know, sweet and eternal God, that you replied earlier to this question—'I am the One who takes delight in few words and many deeds.' Nevertheless, if it may please your goodness to grant me a few more words on the subject, it will cause me the greatest pleasure.

"And also, on some occasion, when I am praying for your creatures, and in particular for your servants, and I seem to see the subjects of my prayer, in one I may find (in the course of my prayer) a well-disposed mind, a soul rejoicing in you. And in another, I may find, as it might seem to me, a mind full of darkness. Do I have the right, eternal Father, to judge one soul to be in light, and the other in darkness?

"Or, supposing I should see that the one lives in great penance, and the other does not. Would I be right to judge that the one who does the greater penance has the higher perfection? I pray you, so that I may not be deceived through my limited vision, that you would declare to me in detail what you have already said in general on this matter.

"The second request I have to make is that you will explain further to me about the sign that you said the soul receives on being visited by you—the sign that reveals your presence. If I remember well, eternal Truth, you said that the soul remains in joy and courageous virtue. I would gladly know whether this joy can consist with the delusion of the passion of spiritual self-love. If it were so, I would humbly confine myself to the sign of virtue.

"These are the things that I beg you to tell me, so that I may serve you and my neighbor in truth, and not fall into false judgment concerning your creatures and servants. It seems to me that the habit of judging keeps the soul far from you, so I do not wish to fall into this snare."

How the light of reason is necessary to every
soul that wishes to serve God in truth; and first
of the light of reason in general.

Then the eternal God, delighting in the thirst and hunger of that servant, and in the purity of her heart, and in the desire with which she longed to serve him, turned the eye of his kindness and mercy upon her, and said—"Best-beloved, dearest and sweetest daughter, my spouse! Rise out of yourself and open the eye of your intellect to see me, the infinite goodness, and the inexpressible love that I have toward you and my other servants. And open the ear of the desire that you feel toward me, and remember, that if you do not see, you cannot hear. That is, the soul who does not see into my truth with the eye of its intellect cannot hear or know my Truth. Therefore, so that you may know it better, rise above the feelings of your senses.

"And I, who take delight in your request, will satisfy your demand. Not that you can increase my delight—for I am the cause of you and of your increase of delight, not you of mine. Yet the very pleasure that I take in the work of my own hands causes me delight."

Then that soul obeyed and rose out of herself, in order to learn the true solution of her difficulty. And the eternal God said to her, "So that you may understand better what I shall say to you, I shall revert to the beginning of your request concerning the three lights that issue from me, the true Light. The first is a general light dwelling in those who live in ordinary charity. The other two lights dwell in those who, having abandoned the world, desire perfection.

"You know that without the light, no one can walk in the truth—that is, without the light of reason. And that light you draw from me, the true light, by means of the eye of your intellect and the light of faith that I have given you in holy baptism—though you may have lost it by your own defects. For, in baptism, and through the mediation of the blood of my only-begotten Son, you have received the form of faith. You exercise faith in virtue by the light of reason, which gives you life and causes you to walk in the path of truth. By means of it you arrive at me, the true light. Without it, you would plunge into darkness.

"It is necessary for you to have two lights derived from this primary light, and to these two I will also add a third. The first lightens you to know the transitory nature of the things of the world, all of which pass like the wind. But this you cannot know thoroughly unless you first recognize your own fragility. You must know how strong is your inclination, through the law of perversity with which your members are bound, to rebel against me, your creator. (Not that by this law anyone can be constrained to commit even the smallest sin against his will—but this law of perversity fights lustily against the spirit.)

"I did not impose this law upon you so that my rational creature should be conquered by it, but so he should prove and increase the virtue of his soul. For virtue cannot be proved, except by its opposite.

"Sensuality is contrary to the spirit, and yet, by means of sensuality, the soul is able to prove the love that it has for me, its creator. How does it prove it? When, with anger and displeasure, it rises against itself. This law has also been imposed in order to preserve the soul in true humility.

"Therefore you see that, while I created the soul in my own image and likeness, placing it in such dignity and beauty, I caused it to be accompanied by the vilest of all things, imposing on it the law of perversity. I imprisoned it in a body, formed of the vilest substance of the earth, so that, seeing in what its true beauty consisted, it should not raise its head in pride against me. Wherefore, to one who possesses this light, the fragility of his body is a cause of humiliation to the soul, and is in no way matter for pride, but rather for true and perfect humility. So this law does not constrain you to any sin by its strivings, but supplies a reason to make you know yourselves and the instability of the world.

"This should be seen by the eye of the intellect, with the light of holy faith, which is the pupil of the eye. This is the light that is necessary to every rational creature, whatever may be his condition, who wishes to participate in the life of grace, in the fruit of the blood of the immaculate Lamb.

"This is the ordinary light, that is, the light that all persons must possess. For, without it, the soul would be in a state of damnation. This is because the soul, being without the light, is not in a state of grace. For, not having the light, it knows neither the evil of its sin nor the cause of its sin, and therefore cannot avoid or hate it.

"And similarly, if the soul does not know good and the reason for good, that is to say virtue, it cannot love or desire me, who am the essential good. Nor can it love or desire virtue, which I have given you as an instrument and means for you to receive both my grace and myself, the true good.

"See then how necessary is this light, for your sins consist in nothing else than in loving what I hate, and in hating what I love. I love virtue and hate vice. One who loves vice and hates virtue offends me and is deprived of my grace. Such a one walks as if blind, for he knows not the cause of vice, that is, his sensual self-love, nor does he hate himself on account of it. He is ignorant of vice and of the evil that follows it. He is ignorant of virtue and of me, who am the cause of his obtaining life-giving virtue. And he is ignorant of his own dignity, which he should maintain by advancing to grace, by means of virtue. See, therefore, how his ignorance is the cause of all his evil, and how you also need this light."

Of those who have placed their desire in the mortification of the body rather than in the destruction of their own will; and of the second light, which is more perfect than the general one.

When the soul has arrived at the attainment of the general light, of which I have spoken, it should not remain contented. For as long as you are pilgrims in this life, you are capable of growth. One who does not go forward, by that very fact, is turning back. The soul should either grow in the general light, which it has acquired through my grace, or strive anxiously to attain to the second and perfect light. For, if the soul truly has light, it will wish to arrive at perfection.

"In this second, perfect light are to be found two kinds of perfection. One perfection is that of those who give themselves up wholly to the castigation of the body, doing great and severe penance. These, so that their sensuality may not rebel against their reason, have placed their desire in the mortification of the body rather than in the destruction of their self-will. They feed their souls at the table of penance, and are good and perfect. And this is true provided that they act with true knowledge of themselves and of me, with great humility, and wholly conformed to the judgment of my will, and not to that of the will of man.

"But, if such souls were not clothed with my will, in true humility, they would often offend against their own perfection, esteeming themselves the judges of those who do not walk in the same path. Do you know why this would happen to them? Because they have placed all their labor and desire in the mortification of the body, rather than in the destruction of their own will. Such as these always wish to choose their own times, and places, and consolations, after their own fashion, and also the persecutions of the world and of the devil.

"They say, cheating themselves with the delusion of their own self-will, which I have already called their spiritual self-will, 'I wish to have that consolation, and not these battles, or these temptations of the devil. Not, indeed, for my own pleasure, but in order to please God the more, and in order to retain him the more in my soul through grace. For it seems to me that I should possess him more, and serve him better in that way than in this.'

"And this is the way the soul often falls into trouble, and becomes tedious and intolerable to itself, thus injuring its own perfection. Yet it does not perceive that within it lurks the stench of pride, and there it lies.

"Now, if the soul were not in this condition, but were truly humble and not presumptuous, it would be illuminated to see that I, the primary and sweet Truth, grant condition, and time, and place, and consolations, and tribulations as they may be needed for your salvation, and to complete the perfection to which I have elected the soul. And it would see that I give everything through love, and that therefore, it should receive everything with love and reverence.

"This is what the souls in the second state do, and, by doing so, they arrive at the third state. I will now speak to you of these souls, explaining to you the nature of these two states that stand in the most perfect light."

Of the third and most perfect state, and of reason,
and of the works done by the soul who has arrived at this light.
And of a beautiful vision that this devout servant of God once
received, in which the method of arriving at perfect purity is fully
treated. And of the means to avoid judging our neighbor.

"Those who belong to the third state, which immediately follows the last, having arrived at this glorious light, are perfect in every condition in which they may be. They receive every event that I permit to happen to them with due reverence. These deem themselves worthy of the troubles and stumbling-blocks that the world causes them, and of the privation of their own consolation, and indeed of whatever circumstance happens to them.

"And inasmuch as these souls deem themselves worthy of trouble, so also do they deem themselves unworthy of the fruit that they receive after their trouble. They have known and tasted in the light my eternal will, which desires nothing but your good.

It gives and permits these troubles in order that you should be sanctified in me.

"Therefore the soul, having known my will, clothes itself with it. It fixes its attention on nothing else except seeing in what way it can preserve and increase its perfection to the glory and praise of my name. It opens the eye of its intellect and fixes it in the light of faith upon Christ crucified, my only-begotten Son. It loves and follows his doctrine, which is the rule for the perfect and imperfect alike.

"Then my Truth, the Lamb, who became enamored of this soul when he saw it, gives it the doctrine of perfection. The soul knows what this perfection is, having seen it practiced by the sweet and amorous Word, my only-begotten Son.

"For my Son was fed at the table of holy desire and sought the honor of me, the eternal Father, and your salvation. Inflamed with this desire, he ran, with great eagerness, to the shameful death of the cross, and accomplished the obedience imposed on him by me, his Father. He shunned neither labors nor insults, nor withdrew on account of your ingratitude or ignorance of so great a benefit. Neither did he withdraw because of the persecutions of the Jews, or on account of the insults, derision, grumbling, and shouting of the people.

"But all this he passed through like the true captain and knight that he was. For I placed him on the battlefield to deliver you from the hands of the devil, so that you might be freed from the most terrible slavery in which you could ever be. And I gave him to you to teach you his road, his doctrine, and his rule, so that you might open the door of me, eternal Life, with the key of his precious blood, shed with such fire of love, with such hatred of your sins.

"It was as if the sweet and loving Word, my Son, had said to you: 'Behold, I have made the road, and opened the door with my blood.' Do not then be negligent to follow. Do not lie down to rest in self-love and ignorance of the road, presuming to choose to serve me in your own way, instead of in the way that I have made straight for you by means of my Truth, the incarnate Word, and built up with his blood. Rise up then, promptly, and follow him, for no one can reach me, the Father, if not by him. He is the way and the door by which you must enter into me, the Sea of Peace.

"When therefore the soul has arrived at seeing, knowing, and tasting this light in its full sweetness, it runs, as one inflamed with love, to the table of holy desire. Like one who has placed his all in this light and knowledge and has destroyed his own will, it shuns no labor, from whatever source it comes. It endures the troubles, the insults, the temptations of the devil, and the murmurings of men. It eats at the table of the most holy cross, the food of the honor of me, the eternal God, and of the salvation of souls.

"It seeks no reward, either from me or from creatures, because it is stripped of mercenary love, that is, of love for me based on self-interested motives. It is clothed in perfect light and loves me in perfect purity, with no other regard than for the praise and glory of my name. It serves neither me for its own delight, nor its neighbor for its own profit, but purely through love alone.

"Such as these have lost themselves, and have stripped themselves of the Old Man, that is, of their own sensuality. Having clothed themselves with the New Man, the sweet Christ Jesus, my Truth, they follow him manfully.

"These sit at the table of holy desire, having been more anxious to slay their own will than to slay and mortify their own body.

They have indeed mortified their body, though not as an end in itself, but as a means to help them keep their own will at bay. Their principal desire should be to slay their own will, so that it may not seek or wish anything else than to follow my sweet Truth, Christ crucified, and to seek the honor and glory of my name and the salvation of souls.

"Those who are in this sweet light know it, and remain constantly in peace and quiet. No one scandalizes them, for they have cut away that thing by which stumbling-blocks are caused, namely their own will. And all the persecutions with which the world and the devil can attack them, slide under their feet and do not hurt them. For they remain attached to me by the umbilical cord of fiery desire.

"Such a one rejoices in everything, and does not make himself judge of my servants or of any rational creature. Rather, he rejoices in every condition and in every manner of holiness that he sees, saying: 'Thanks be to you, eternal Father, who have in your house many mansions.'

"And he rejoices more in the different ways of holiness that he sees than if he were to see everyone traveling by one road. He finds, in this way, that he perceives the greatness of my goodness become more manifest. Thus, rejoicing, he draws from everything the fragrance of the rose.

"And not only in the case of good, but even when he sees something evidently sinful he does not fall into judgment. Rather, he shows true and holy compassion and intercedes with me for sinners. And he says, with perfect humility: 'Today it is your turn, and tomorrow it will be mine, unless divine grace preserves me.'

"Dearest daughter, love this sweet and excellent state. Gaze at those who run in this glorious light and holiness, for they have holy minds, and eat at the table of holy desire. They have arrived at feeding on the food of souls, that is, the honor of me, the eternal Father. And they are clothed with burning love in the sweet garment of my Lamb, my only-begotten Son, namely his doctrine. These do not lose their time in passing false judgments, either on my servants or the servants of the world. And they are never scandalized by any murmurings of men, either for their own sake or that of others.

"And since their love is so ordered, these souls, my dearest daughter, never take offense at those they love, nor at any rational creature, for their will is dead and not alive. They never assume the right to judge the will of men, but only the will of my clemency.

"These souls observe the doctrine that was given you by my Truth at the beginning of your life, when you were thinking in what way you could arrive at perfect purity, and were praying to me with a great desire of doing so. You know what I replied to you, while you were asleep, concerning this holy desire. And you know that the words resounded not only in your mind, but also in your ear. So much so, that you returned to your waking body.

"And my Truth said, 'Will you arrive at perfect purity, and be freed from stumbling-blocks, so that your mind may not be scandalized by anything? Unite yourself always to me by the affection of love, for I am the supreme and eternal purity. I am the fire that purifies the soul. The closer the soul is to me, the purer it becomes. And the farther it is from me, the more its purity leaves it.'

"The reason persons of the world fall into such iniquities is that they are separated from me. But the soul who, without any medium, unites itself directly to me, participates in my purity.

"Another thing is necessary for you to arrive at this union and purity, namely, you should never judge the will of man in anything that you may see done or said by any creature whatsoever, either to yourself or to others. You should consider my will alone, both in them and in yourself. And if you should see evidence of sins or defects, draw the rose out of those thorns. That is, offer them to me, with holy compassion.

"In the case of injuries done to you, judge that my will permits them in order to prove virtue in you and in my other servants. Esteem that one who acts in an injurous manner does so as the instrument of my will. Such apparent sinners may frequently have good intentions, for no one can judge the secrets of the heart of man. What you do not see you should not judge in your mind, even though externally it may be open, mortal sin.

"See nothing in others but my will, not in order to judge, but with holy compassion. In this way you will arrive at perfect purity. For, acting in this way, your mind will not be scandalized either in me or by your neighbor. Otherwise you fall into contempt of your neighbor if you judge his evil will toward you, instead of acknowledging my will acting in him.

"Such contempt and scandal separates the soul from me and prevents perfection. And, in some cases, it deprives a person of grace, more or less according to the gravity of his contempt and the hatred that his judgment has conceived against his neighbor.

"A different reward is received by the soul who perceives only my will, which wishes nothing else but your good. Everything I give or permit to happen to you, I give so that you may arrive at the end for which I created you. And because the soul remains always in the love of its neighbor, it remains always in mine, and thus it remains united to me.

"Therefore, in order to arrive at purity, you must entreat me to grant you three things: First, to be united to me by the affection of love, retaining in your memory the benefits you have received from me. Second, with the eye of your intellect to see the affection of my love, with which I love you inestimably. And third, in the will of others to discern my will only, and not their evil will. For I am their judge, not you. And in doing this, you will arrive at all perfection.

"This was the doctrine given to you by my Truth. Now I tell you, dearest daughter, that those who have learned this doctrine taste the pledge of eternal life in this life. And, if you have retained this doctrine well, you will not fall into the snares of the devil, because you will recognize them in the case about which you have asked me.

"But nevertheless, in order to satisfy your desire more clearly, I will tell you and show you how men should never discern by judgment, but with holy compassion."

*In what way those who stand in the third and most perfect
light receive the pledge of eternal life while in this life.*

"Why did I say to you that they received the pledge of eternal life? I say that they receive the pledge, but not the full payment, because they wait to receive it in me, who am eternal Life. In me they have life without death, and are filled, but not to excess. In me they have hunger without pain, for from that divine hunger, pain is far away. Though they have what they desire, their fulfillment contains no excess, for I am the flawless food of life.

"It is true that in this life they receive the pledge and taste it in that the soul begins to hunger for the honor of the eternal God and for the food of the salvation of other souls. And being hungry, it eats. That is, it nourishes itself with love of its neighbor, which causes its hunger and desire. For the love of one's neighbor is a food that never fills to excess the one who feeds on it. Thus the eater cannot be completely filled and always remains hungry.

"So this pledge is the commencement of a guarantee that is given to mankind. In virtue of this pledge he expects one day to receive his payment. His expectation is not based on the perfection of the pledge in itself, but on faith, on the certainty that he has of reaching the completion of his being and receiving his payment.

"Therefore this loving soul, clothed in my truth, has already received in this life the pledge of my love and of its neighbor's. This soul is not yet perfect, but awaits perfection in immortal life.

"I say that this pledge is not perfect, because the soul who tastes it does not yet have the perfection that would prevent its feeling pain in itself or in others: in itself through the offense done to me by the law of perversity that is bound in its members and struggles against the spirit; and in others by the offense of its neighbor.

"The soul has indeed, in a sense, a perfect grace. But it does not have that perfection of my saints, those who have arrived at me, who am eternal Life. For their desires are without suffering, and yours are not. These servants of mine, who nourish themselves at this table of holy desire, are both blessed and full of grief, even as my only-begotten Son was on the wood of the holy cross. There, while his flesh was in grief and torment, his soul was blessed through its union with the divine nature.

"In like manner these servants are blessed by the union of their holy desire toward me. They are clothed in my sweet will. And they are full of grief through compassion for their neighbor, and because they afflict their own self-love, depriving it of sensual delights and consolations."

How this servant of God, rendering thanks to God,
humbles herself; then she prays for the whole world
and particularly for the mystical body of
the holy church and for her spiritual children,
and for the two fathers of her soul; and, after
these things, she asks to hear something about the defects of the
ministers of the holy church.

Then that servant of God, as if actually intoxicated, seemed beside herself. It was as if the feelings of her body were alienated through the union of love that she had made with her creator. And it was as if, in elevating her mind, she had gazed into the eternal truth with the eye of her intellect, and, having recognized the truth, had become deeply in love with it.

And she said, "Supreme one! You, Supreme and eternal Father, have manifested to me your truth, the hidden deceits of the devil, and the deceitfulness of personal feeling. You have done this so that I, and others in this life of pilgrimage, may know how to avoid being deceived by the devil or ourselves! What moved you to do so? Love, because you loved me without my having loved you.

"Fire of Love! Thanks, thanks be to you, eternal Father! I am imperfect and full of darkness, and you, perfection and light, have shown to me perfection and the resplendent way of the doctrine of your only-begotten Son.

"I was dead, and you have brought me to life. I was sick, and you have given me medicine. And yours was not only the medicine of the Blood that you gave for the diseased human race in the person of your Son, but also a medicine against a secret infirmity of which I was unaware.

"For you have shown me that in no way can I judge any rational creature, and particularly your servants, upon whom I often passed judgment under the pretext of your honor and the salvation of souls. Therefore, I thank you, supreme and eternal good, that, in manifesting your truth, the deceitfulness of the devil, and our own passions, you have made me know my infirmity.

"Therefore I beseech you through grace and mercy that, from today forward, I may never again wander from the path of your doctrine, which was given by your goodness to me and to whoever wishes to follow it. And I beseech you to grant this because without you is nothing done. To you, then, eternal Father, I have recourse and flee.

"I do not beseech you for myself alone, Father, but for the whole world, and particularly for the mystical body of the holy church, that this truth given to me, miserable one that I am, by you, eternal truth, may shine in your ministers.

"Also I beseech you especially for all those whom you have given me, and whom you have made one with me, and whom I love with a particular love. For they will be my refreshment to the glory and praise of your name, when I see them running on this sweet and straight road, pure, and dead to their own will and opinion, and without passing any judgment on their neighbor or causing him any scandal or murmuring. And I pray you, sweetest love, that not one of them may be taken from me by the hand of the infernal devil, so that at last they may arrive at you, their end, eternal Father.

"I now know for certain, eternal Truth, that you will not despise the desire of the petitions that I have made to you, because I know, from seeing what it has pleased you to manifest, and still more from proof, that you are the acceptor of holy desires. I, your unworthy servant, will strive, according as you will give me grace, to observe your commandments and your doctrine.

"Now, eternal Father, I remember a word that you said to me in speaking of the ministers of the holy church, to the effect that you would speak to me more distinctly, in some other place, of the sins that they commit today. If it should please your goodness to tell me anything of this matter, I will gladly hear it, so as to have material for increasing my grief, compassion, and anxious desire for their salvation. I remember that you said that, on account of the endurance, the tears, the grief, the sweat, and the prayers of your servants, you would reform the holy church, and comfort her with good and holy pastors. I ask you this so that these sentiments may increase in me."

How God renders this soul attentive to prayer,
replying to one of the above-mentioned petitions.

Then the eternal God turned the eye of his mercy upon this servant. Not despising her desire, but granting her requests, he proceeded to satisfy the last petition that she had made concerning his promise, saying, "Best beloved and dearest daughter, I will fulfill your desire in this request, so that, on your side, you may not sin through ignorance or negligence. For a fault of yours would be more serious and worthy of graver reproof now than before, because you have learned more of my truth.

"Apply yourself attentively to pray for all rational creatures, for the mystical body of the holy church, and for those friends whom I have given you, whom you love with particular love. And be careful not to be negligent in giving them the benefit of your prayers, the example of your life, and the teaching of your words, reproving vice and encouraging virtue according to your power.

"Concerning the supports that I have given you, of whom you spoke to me, know that you are truly a means by which they may each receive, according to their needs and fitness. And I, your creator, grant you this opportunity, for without me you can do nothing. I will fulfill your desires, but do not fail, or they either, in your hope in me. And my providence will never fail you.

"So every person, if he is humble, shall receive what he is fit to receive. And every minister shall receive what I have given him to administer, each in his own way, according to what he has received and will receive from my goodness."

How this devout servant, praising and thanking God,
made a prayer for the holy church.

Then this servant, as if intoxicated, tormented, and on fire with love, her heart wounded with great bitterness, turned to the supreme and eternal goodness, and said: "Eternal God!

Light above every other light! Fire above every fire! You are the only fire that burns without consuming, and you consume all sin and self-love found in the soul. You do not afflict the soul, but you fatten it with insatiable love. And though the soul is filled it is not sated. The more of you it has, the more it seeks. And the more it desires, the more it finds and tastes of you, supreme and eternal fire, abyss of charity.

"Supreme and eternal good, who has moved you, infinite God, to illuminate me, your finite creature, with the light of your truth? You, the same fire of love, are the cause. For it is love that has always constrained and continues to constrain you to create us in your image and likeness, and to show us mercy by giving immeasurable and infinite graces to your rational creatures.

"Goodness above all goodness! You alone are supremely good, and nevertheless you gave the Word, your only-begotten Son, to associate with us filthy ones who are filled with darkness. What was the cause of this? Love. Because you loved us before we were.

"Eternal greatness! You made yourself low and small to make mankind great. On whichever side I turn I find nothing but the abyss and fire of your love. And can a wretch like me pay back to you the graces and the burning love that you have shown and continue to show in particular to me, and the love that you show to all your creatures? No, but you alone, most sweet and loving Father, will be thankful and grateful for me—that is, that the affection of your charity itself will render you thanks. My being, and every further grace that you have bestowed upon me, I have from you. And you give them to me through love, and not as my due.

"Sweetest Father, when the human race lay sick through the sin of Adam, you sent it a physician, the sweet and loving

Word—Your Son. And when I was lying infirm with the sickness of negligence and much ignorance, you, most soothing and sweet physician, eternal God, gave a soothing, sweet, and bitter medicine, that I may be cured and rise from my infirmity. You soothed me because with your love and gentleness you manifested yourself to me, sweet above all sweetness. You illuminated the eye of my intellect with the light of most holy faith.

"As it has pleased you to manifest your light to me, I have known the excellence of grace that you have given to the human race. For you administer to it the entire God-Man in the mystical body of the holy church. And I have known the dignity of your ministers, whom you have appointed to administer you to us. I desired that you would fulfill the promise that you made to me, and you gave much more, more even than I knew how to ask for.

"Therefore I know in truth that the human heart does not know how to ask or desire as much as you can give. And thus I see that you are the supreme and eternal good, and that we are not. And because you are infinite, and we are finite, you give what your rational creatures cannot desire enough, filling us with things for which we do not ask you.

"Moreover, I have received light from your greatness and charity, through the love that you have for the whole human race, and in particular for your anointed ones, who ought to be earthly angels in this life. You have shown me the virtue and the blessed state of these your anointed ones, who have lived like burning lamps, shining with the pearl of justice in the holy church.

"And by comparison with these I have better understood the sins of those who live wretchedly. Therefore I have conceived a very great sorrow at offenses done to you, and at the harm done to the whole world. And because you have manifested and grieved over their iniquities—to me, a wretch who am the cause and instrument of many sins—I am plunged into intolerable grief.

"You, inestimable love, have manifested this to me, giving me a sweet and bitter medicine. You have done this so that I might wholly arise out of the infirmity of my ignorance and negligence, knowing myself and your goodness and the offenses that are committed against you. And you have desired that I might shed a river of tears over my wretched self and over those who are dead, in that they live miserably.

"Therefore I do not wish, eternal Father, inexpressible fire of love, that my heart should ever grow weary, or my eyes fail through tears, in desiring your honor and the salvation of souls. But I beg of you, by your grace, that these may be as two streams of water issuing from you, the Sea of Peace.

"Thanks, thanks to you, Father, for granting me what I asked you and what I neither knew nor asked. For by thus giving me matter for grief you have invited me to offer before you sweet, loving, and yearning desires, with humble and continual prayer. Now I beg of you to show mercy to the world and to the holy church. I pray you to fulfill what you caused me to ask you.

"Alas! what a wretched and sorrowful soul is mine, the cause of all these evils. Do not put off any longer your merciful designs toward the world, but descend and fulfill the desire of your servants.

"I know well that mercy is your own attribute, and thus you can not destroy it or refuse it to one who asks for it. Your servants knock at the door of your truth, because in the truth of your only-begotten Son they know the inexpressible love that you have for mankind. As a result, the fire of your love ought not and cannot refrain from opening to one who knocks with perseverance.

"Therefore open, unlock, and break the hardened hearts of your creatures, not for their sakes who do not knock, but on account of your infinite goodness. Grant the prayer of those, eternal Father, who, as you see, stand at the door of your truth and pray. For what do they pray? For with the blood of this door—your Truth—you have washed our iniquities and destroyed the stain of Adam's sin. The blood is ours, for you have made it our bath, and thus you cannot deny it to any one who truly asks for it.

"Give, then, the fruit of your blood to your creatures. Place in the balance the price of the blood of your Son, so that the infernal devils may not carry off your lambs. You are the good shepherd who, to fulfill your obedience, lay down his life for your lambs, and made for us a bath of his blood.

"That blood is what your hungry servants beg of you at this door. They beg you through it to show mercy to the world, and to cause your holy church to bloom with the fragrant flowers of good and holy pastors, who by their sweet odor shall extinguish the stench of the putrid flowers of sin.

"You have said, eternal Father, that through the love that you have for your rational creatures, and the prayers and the many virtues and labors of your servants, you would show mercy to the world and reform the church, and thus give us refreshment. Therefore do not delay, but turn the eye of your mercy toward us, for you must first reply to us before we can cry out with the voice of your mercy.

"Open the door of your inestimable love, which you have given us through the door of your Word. I know indeed that you open before we can even knock. For it is with the affection of love that you have given to your servants, that they knock and cry to you, seeking your honor and the salvation of souls.

"Give them then the bread of life, that is to say, the fruit of the blood of your only-begotten Son, which they ask of you for the praise and glory of your name and the salvation of souls. For more glory and praise will be yours in saving so many creatures, than in leaving them obstinate in their hardness of heart.

"To you, eternal Father, everything is possible, and even though you have created us without our own help, you will not save us without it. I beg of you to force their wills, and to dispose them to wish for that for which they do not wish. And this I ask you through your infinite mercy.

"You have created us from nothing. Now, therefore, that we are in existence, show mercy to us, and remake the vessels that you have created in your image and likeness. Re-create them to grace in your mercy and in the blood of your Son, sweet Christ Jesus."

THE CLOUD OF UNKNOWING

CHAPTER 3
A superior discipline

Let modest love prompt you to lift up your heart to God. Seek only God. Think of nothing else other than God. Keep your mind free of other thoughts. Give no attention to the things of this world.

These pages describe spiritual contemplation that is pleasing to God. When the saints and angels observe you in this state, they rush to help you. Devils will be disturbed when you begin, and they will use all their tricks to discourage you. In a mysterious way, your contemplation of God helps others even as it helps you.

Contemplation is not difficult or complex. Enthusiastic desire will accomplish much. With God's gift of spiritual hunger, you will make steady progress. Continue until your prayer life becomes enjoyable.

When you begin, you will experience a darkness, a *cloud of unknowing*. You cannot interpret this darkness. You will only comprehend a basic reaching out toward God. None of your efforts will remove the cloud that obscures God from your understanding. Darkness will remain between you and the love of God. You will feel nothing.

Accept this dark cloud. Learn to live with it, but keep looking, praying, and crying out to the one you love. Any insight you ever gain of God while you live in this world will be in this cloud and in this darkness. If you will continue in the manner I describe, I believe that God, in his good pleasure, will grant you an instant of profound religious experience.

CHAPTER 4
Knowledge and imagination

I do not want you to have misconceptions regarding the contemplative work of the soul. Therefore, let me describe in detail what I have learned about this plain and simple practice.

Many think contemplative prayer takes a long time to achieve. On the contrary, results may be instantaneous. Only an atom of time, as we perceive it, may pass. In this fraction of a second, something profoundly significant happens. You only need a tiny scrap of time to move toward God. This brief moment produces the stirring that embodies the greatest work of your soul. How many desires can fill an hour? You may have as many desires as there are indivisible fractions of time in an hour.

If you were as sinless as Adam was before the fall, you would be in total control of each instant. You would respond to every divine impulse. Everything about you would reach toward God all the time, because God created us in his image. In the Incarnation, Christ emptied himself, becoming one of us, accommodating himself to our limitations. Only God satisfies our spiritual hunger. Nothing else suffices. After God graciously transforms our soul, we begin perceiving what is ordinarily beyond our comprehension. Angels do not have the mental capacity, nor do we, to grasp the total reality of God, but what cannot be ours by intelligence can be ours as we embrace love.

Every rational creature has both the power of knowing and the power of loving. Our Creator endows us with both, but God will forever remain incomprehensible to the knowing power. Through loving power, however, each of us may know God. Love is everlastingly miraculous. May God help you to understand what I mean, because endless joy waits for you.

If God were to bless you with absolute control of your will, you would have a constant awareness of heavenly bliss. My enthusiasm should not surprise you. God designed us for this. God created us to love, and everything else in God's creation helps you love. The exercise explained in this book will restore our spiritual consciousness, but if we neglect prayerful contemplation, we sink ever deeper into unawareness.

Pay attention, then, to how you spend your time. You have nothing more precious than time. In one tiny moment of time, heaven may be gained or lost. God gives us time in sequence, one instant after another and never simultaneously. We only experience the present moment. God never reverses the orderly progression of time. God does not ask for more than we can handle in one moment.

I can almost hear you expressing regret. "What can I do? If what you say is true, how can I account for each moment God has already given me? I am now twenty-four years old and I haven't paid any attention to how I used my time. Even if I wanted to, I could not repair any past moment. The past remains as far beyond my reach as the future. Will tomorrow be any different? My own spiritual slowness traps me. For the love of Jesus, please help me."

You used the correct expression when you said "for the love of Jesus." The love of Jesus is the source of the help you need. Love's power brings everything together. Love Jesus, and everything of his becomes yours. As God made time, so God judges our use of time. Tie yourself to him with love and faith, knitting your relationship together. This way you may become a part of the larger fellowship of those fastened to God by love. You will have friends among the saints and angels who do not waste any time.

Pay attention and you will discover strength here. Try to understand what I am saying. But I offer one caution. You will not arrive at this relationship passively. God demands your personal involvement and dedication. Apply yourself diligently to both prayer and community responsibilities.

Notice, then, how contemplation affects your own soul. Genuine contemplation comes as a spontaneous, unexpected moment, a sudden springing toward God that shoots like a spark swirling up from a burning coal. A remarkable number of such moments may occur in an hour when the person in contemplation prepares properly and becomes familiar with this work. Any one of these sparkling moments may take on a unique quality resulting in a total detachment from the things of this world. On the other hand, earthly responsibilities and intrusions may tear you away from prayer. The thoughts of frail humans distract attention. Accept this as a natural experience. Your spiritual life receives no harm because of it. With practice, you may return immediately to profound prayer as another spark springs from the fire.

I have briefly summarized this experience of contemplation. Clearly, I report something quite different from fantasy, imagination, or subtle reasoning. Daydreaming is not the result of humble, devout love. A proud, speculative, and hyper-imaginative mind results in religious pretense. Control and subdue such elaborate notions.

Whoever reads or hears the directions given in this book may conclude that I am describing mental effort. But taxing your brain in an attempt to figure ways to achieve this produces nothing. Intellectual curiosity will lead you to dangerous self-deception. Unless God mercifully pulls you away from such a course, you may quickly fall into harmful frenzies and other spiritual sins that are works of the devil. May God lead you to an experienced, competent spiritual director who can guide you. For the love of God, be careful when you attempt contemplative prayer. Leave your senses and your imagination at rest, because there is no function for them here.

When I refer to this exercise as "darkness" or a "cloud," do not compare it with the darkness in your house when the candle burns out, or with a cloud in the sky that is composed of water vapor. Anyone can imaginatively conceive of that kind of darkness and cloud, even in broad daylight. I am not talking about such things.

Darkness results from a lack of knowledge, something unknown to you. What obscures God from you is not a cloud in the sky, but the *cloud of unknowing*.

CHAPTER 5
The cloud of forgetting

If you want to enter, live, and work in this *cloud of unknowing*, you will need a *cloud of forgetting* between you and the things of this earth. Consider the problem carefully and you will understand that you are farthest from God when you do not ignore for a moment the creatures and circumstances of the physical world. Attempt to blank out everything but God.

Even valuable thoughts of some special creatures are of little use for this exercise. Memory is a kind of spiritual light that the eye of the soul focuses upon, similar to the way an archer fixes his gaze upon a target. I tell you, whatever you think about looms above you while you are thinking about it, and it stands between you and God. To the extent that anything other than God is in your mind, you are that much farther from God.

I will also say, with reverence and respect, that regarding this exercise, even thinking about the kindness and worthiness of God, of any other spiritual being, or of the joys of heaven contributes nothing. These are uplifting and worthy subjects, but you are far better off contemplating God's pure and simple being, separated from all his divine attributes.

CHAPTER 6
A brief dialogue

You ask me, "How can I think about God in this elemental way?"

I reply, "I don't know. Your question has wrapped me in the same darkness, that *cloud of unknowing*, I wish you were in. It is possible for us to have extensive knowledge of many subjects, even theology. We have no difficulty thinking about such things. But we are incapable of thinking of God himself with our inadequate minds. Let us abandon everything within the scope of our thoughts and determine to love what is beyond comprehension. We touch and hold God by love alone.

"Therefore, while thinking about God's kindness and holiness may sometimes be worthwhile, these thoughts must be subdued (covered with a *cloud of forgetting*) in your time of contemplation. Have the courage to step above such ideas with loving devotion. Pierce that thick *cloud of unknowing* with a sharp dart of longing love. Do not turn away no matter what happens."

CHAPTER 7
Intellectual curiosity

Suppose a thought nags your mind, placing itself between you and that darkness, asking you, "What do you want? Whom do you seek?" Give this answer: "I want God. I am looking for God, only God."

And if the thought persists, asking you, "Who is the God you seek?" answer saying, "The God who made me, redeemed me, and led me to this moment." Speak to your mind, "Thoughts, you cannot contain God. You have limited skill and you offer no assistance. Be silent!" Ignore the activity of your mind by devoutly turning to Jesus, even if your thoughts appear to be holy thoughts.

Quite likely, you will imagine your ideas are helpful. Many excellent and wonderful aspects of Christ's kindness, graciousness, and mercy spring up in your mind. They appear positive and worthy of your consideration, but as the mental chatter continues, it drags you down lower and lower, diverting your attention. Remember the Passion of Christ. This will lead you to recall your sinful past life. Memories of earlier times and places will flood into your awareness, scattering you in many directions; your concentration will be lost. This happened because you deliberately listened, responded, accepted, and allowed the thought to continue.

Still, these may be good and holy thoughts, essential elements as you begin meditation. You need to ponder frequently your own wretchedness, the Passion of Christ, and the kindness, extraordinary goodness, and dignity of God. Unless you do this, frustration will disturb your contemplation. With experience, you will learn to let distracting thoughts rest under a *cloud of forgetting* and attempt to penetrate the *cloud of unknowing* separating you from God.

Therefore, when God leads you to engage in the exercise described here, gently lift up your heart to God with love. Rest your thoughts only on the God who created you, redeemed you, and led you to this moment. Avoid any other thoughts of God. Direct a naked desire toward God.

You may wish to reach out to God with one simple word that expresses your desire. A single syllable is better than a word with two or more. "God" and "love" provide excellent examples of such words. Once you have selected the word you prefer, permanently bind this word to your heart. This word becomes your shield and spear in combat and in peace. Use this word to beat upon the cloudy darkness above you and to force every stray thought down under a *cloud of forgetting*. If a nagging thought pesters you, strike it with this monosyllabic word. If your mind begins to analyze the intellectual ramifications of your chosen word, remember that the value of this word is its simplicity. Do not allow the word to become fragmented. If you keep it intact, I can assure you distractions will soon diminish.

CHAPTER 8
Regarding uncertainties

Now you ask, "How do I evaluate these ideas that intrude upon my meditation? Are they good or evil? I doubt that they are evil, because they serve ordinary devotion so well. These thoughts bring pleasure. I have wept bitterly in sympathy with Christ and sometimes because of my awareness of my own wretched condition; this is a sacred and worthwhile experience. I can't consider such self-knowledge evil. If these thoughts do so much good for me, then why do you instruct me to press them down until they are out of sight beneath a *cloud of forgetting*?"

You ask an excellent question that I will try to answer. You want me to identify and label the thoughts that engage your mind in this exercise. You are thinking clearly, and each idea seems inherently good because you are reflecting the image of God.

Your use of each thought is critically important. The idea becomes good or evil in the application. Good results when God's grace enlightens you, enabling you to perceive your spiritual hunger and the wonderful kindness of God's activity. Your devotion increases. But if the thought makes you proud and arrogant, evil results follow. When you attempt subtle, theological speculation and vainly seek recognition as a scholar, rather than seeking devout humility, then you have lost thinking's most valuable aspect. Anyone who wants to appear clever and knowledgeable in any academic discipline, religious or secular, merely seeks flattery.

You also ask about the value of a *cloud of forgetting*. If such good thoughts assist a spiritual experience, why abandon them? The explanation lies in the difference between active and contemplative Christian living. Both activity and contemplation are essential and interrelated. You cannot fully experience one without the other, even though they have differences in character. The effectively active person is also contemplative. A contemplative person engages in Christian activity. The distinction between the two is that the active life begins and ends in this world, while the contemplative life begins here and continues eternally. Jesus told Martha, who was busy in the kitchen, that her sister, Mary, had chosen what is better, and she would never lose it. Active Martha is troubled and anxious about many things, but contemplative Mary sits in peace, intent only upon him.

At an elemental level, the active life engages in good and honest works of love and mercy. When the active life reaches higher expression, it shares good, spiritual meditation with the lower part of the contemplative life. But the higher part of the contemplative life, to the limited degree it may be experienced here, consists entirely in this darkness and this *cloud of unknowing*. It is an impulse of love, a dark gazing into the pure being of God.

In the beginning of the active life, we look beyond ourselves and work for others. As we progress in Christian activity, we begin to ponder the things of the spirit, but we remain within ourselves. But in the higher degree of the contemplative life, we rise above ourselves. We arrive by grace where we cannot go by nature. We unite with God in spirit, sharing his love, and we are in harmony with God's will.

As we cannot come to the higher part of the active life without pausing our business in the lower part, so we cannot come to the higher degree of the contemplative life without moving away from the elementary stages. Even holy works interfere with meditation. Similarly, you will find it inappropriate and cumbersome to think profound holy thoughts while working in this darkness of the *cloud of unknowing*.

For this reason, I advise you to suppress such pleasant thoughts, covering them with a thick *cloud of forgetting*, regardless of the apparent high quality of your ideas. In this life, love is the only way to reach God. Knowledge does not assist us. As long as the soul lives in this mortal body, the clarity of our understanding in the contemplation of spiritual things, particularly of God, mingles with imagination, tainting the experience and leading us into great error.

CHAPTER 9
Contemplative prayer

Resist intense mental activity when seeking this dark contemplation. Intellectual activity will hinder you. When
you want to be alone with God, the conceptualizations of
your mind will sneak into play. Rather than this darkness,
our intellectual ability prefers a clear picture of something
less than God. Such mental images, as pleasant as they may
be, stand between you and God. Resist them.

For the health of your soul, pleasing God, and helping
others, engage in a blind impulse of love toward God alone,
a secret love beating on this *cloud of unknowing*. Seeking
God this way is superior to seeing all the angels and saints in
heaven, or hearing the laughter and music of those in bliss.

If you experience divine contemplation once on this level,
you will agree I am not exaggerating. There is no way you will
ever have a clear vision of God in this life, but you can have
the gracious feeling I describe, if God grants it. Therefore,
lift up your love to that cloud. More accurately, let God draw
your love up to that cloud. Let God's grace help you to forget
everything other than God. If all you are seeking is God, you
will not be content with anything else.

CHAPTER 10
Discernment

When you are contemplating, thoughts about others fall into another category. Distractions may arrive unconsciously, beyond your control. Such thoughts may result in pleasure or grief. Human nature is frail. Quickly reject these thoughts; otherwise you will begin to experience positive or negative emotional responses and lose your stability. A memory of some pleasant past experience may trigger delight. A painful thought may make you angry.

If you have forsaken the world and committed yourself to a devout life, a temporary lapse does no harm. Root your intentions in God. Lingering with other thoughts allows them to intrude upon your spiritual experience. Consenting to them exposes you to the risk of falling into one of the seven deadly sins. For instance, if you willingly think of someone who has troubled you and you begin to conceive of ways to get even, *wrath* may result. *Envy* follows when you rashly develop a loathing contempt for another person. Or maybe you become weary of a good occupation and want to avoid it. *Sloth* then traps you. If you enjoy thinking about yourself, your achievements and attractiveness, *pride* waits at your elbow. Dwelling on material possessions you wish were yours becomes *covetousness*. If you cannot get your mind off delightful food and drink, you experience *gluttony*. When your thoughts concern the pleasures of love and flattery, or the seduction of another person, you *lust*.

CHAPTER 11
Evaluating thoughts

The purpose of my comments is not to place a burden of guilt on you. I want you to evaluate carefully each thought that stirs in your mind when you contemplate God. If an idea leads to sin, put a stop to it immediately. If you become careless about your early thoughts, you will have greater difficulty later. Everyone sins, but watch out for increasing sinfulness. True disciples can always avoid carelessness. Neglecting simple things prepares you for worse sins.

CHAPTER 12
Results of contemplation

To have a solid footing and to avoid stumbling, consistently puncture the *cloud of unknowing* that is between you and God with a sharp dart of longing love. Avoid thinking of anything less than God, and do not quit your time of contemplation regardless of what may happen. Loving contemplation destroys our tendency to sin more effectively than any other practice. Contemplation is superior to your fasts and vigils, regardless of how early in the morning you get up, the hardness of your bed, or the roughness of your hair shirt. Even if it were lawful for you to blind yourself, cut your tongue from your mouth, plug up your ears and nose, cut off your limbs and become a eunuch, none of these physical tortures would be of any value to you. The impulse to sin would still be in you.

Moreover, regardless of how much you fret about your sins in your straying thoughts or think of the joys of heaven, what do you gain? All of the value you gain from such practices fades when compared with the impulse of love. This, without anything else, is what Jesus described as Mary's "best part." When detached from loving desire, religious practices have little or no spiritual results.

Not only does contemplation destroy, as much as possible, our propensity to sin, it also attracts virtue. You will attract and absorb pure virtue when you truly seek God. Without love, any virtue you may already have will be tainted and imperfect.

Genuine goodness, after all, involves a unified, controlled love for God alone. All virtue is a gift of God, and two virtues, humility and love, include all the others. When we have these two, we have them all.

CHAPTER 13
Perfect and imperfect humility

Perfect humility comes from God. Humility from any other source means imperfection. To understand this, try to comprehend the true nature of humility.

Humility results from an honest personal appraisal. Nothing humbles us more than seeing ourselves clearly. Self-knowledge involves two steps. The first is an admission of our sinful nature. Regardless of our attempts to live a holy life, we cannot escape an awareness of our weak and fallen condition. The other source of our humility results from the recognition of the transcendent love and worthiness of God. Before

God, nature trembles, the most educated become fools, and the saints and angels turn away from the brightness. God's presence inspires awe, and if God did not sustain us during the experience of it, unthinkable things might happen.

Perfect humility results from firsthand experience of God's goodness, and it lasts forever. Imperfect humility that springs from self-evaluation soon passes away, not only when we die, but also during those inspired moments when God allows an individual to rise above self-awareness. Whether this happens frequently or infrequently, it lingers for only a brief moment. During that instant, perfect humility is ours.

I do not intend to denigrate the first motive with the label "imperfect." Do not misinterpret what I am saying. You discover something of importance when you perceive your personal shortcomings.

CHAPTER 14

Begin with imperfect humility

I do not intend to denigrate the importance of honest self-knowledge when I speak of "imperfect" humility. Self-knowledge effectively helps me toward perfect humility, more so than having all the saints and angels in heaven, and having all living Christians pray constantly for me to obtain perfect humility. In fact, perfect humility is impossible without what I call "imperfect" humility.

Therefore, seek true knowledge of yourself. Eventually, you will arrive at a true knowledge and experience of God to the degree allowed to a humble soul still living in a mortal body.

Do not take my two divisions of humility (imperfect and perfect) as a directive to ignore the one and seek the other. I am explaining the extraordinary value of contemplative prayer, and how secret love, lifted in purity of spirit to the dark *cloud of unknowing* that exists between you and God, truly contains perfect humility without any special apprehension of anything less than God. If you know how to identify perfect humility, it becomes a signpost in your awareness. Lack of knowledge often results in pride.

If you do not understand perfect humility, your incomplete knowledge allows you to imagine you have already discovered it. Deceiving yourself, you might think you possess extreme humility while remaining immersed in foul, stinking pride. Strive for perfect humility. When you have it, you will not commit sin. Once you have experienced a moment of perfect humility, you will remain less susceptible to temptation.

CHAPTER 15
Understanding humility

Some mistakenly teach that remembering our despicable sins is the best path to perfect humility. Perfect humility exists, and God may allow you the experience, but introspection is not the best way to receive it.

True, for habitual sinners, a memory of past sins is spiritually useful. We are encrusted by a "rust" of sin. Our conscience and our spiritual director need to scour it away. On the other hand, some people naturally behave well and do not deliberately sin. Their sin is the result of weakness and lack of understanding. And yet, even these almost innocent ones who attempt a life of contemplative prayer have good reason for humility. Motivation toward humility comes from something far above imperfect self-knowledge. The goodness and love of God transcend imperfect motivation. Our Lord Jesus Christ tells us in the Gospel to be perfect by God's grace even as he is perfect by nature.

CHAPTER 16
Contemplative humility

There is no audacity in lovingly reaching out to God in the darkness of that *cloud of unknowing* between you and God. If you repent and experience a call to a life of contemplation, God welcomes you. Jesus told the sinful woman who washed his feet with her tears and dried them with her hair, "Your sins are forgiven." Divine forgiveness was not the result of her great sorrow, or her conviction of sin, or her perception of her own wretchedness. The Scripture tells us that Jesus said it because "she loved much." Study this biblical incident and see what a hidden impulse of love can elicit from our Lord.

Now there is no doubt that she regretted her sins and felt humility. Her deep sorrow was bundled together and carried perpetually in the recesses of her heart. She could never forget her sins. And yet, Scripture affirms that she had a greater sorrow provoked by her lack of love. She languished with sorrowing desire, sighing deeply, though her love was already strong. This should not surprise us, because the more we love, the more we want to love.

What did she do? Did she move down from the heights of her great desire and wallow in the memory of her failures? Did she search under every stone in the foul-smelling bog and dunghill of her life history? Did she dredge up her sins, one by one, sorrowing and weeping over each? No. Absolutely not. Why? Because God helped her to understand, by the grace in her soul, that this would not help anything.

She did the very opposite. She hung up her love and her longing desire in this *cloud of unknowing* and attempted to learn to love something she might never clearly perceive in this life, neither by intellectual insight nor by a true feeling of sweet, affectionate love. As a result, she paid little attention to whether or not she had been a sinner. The Lord's divinity moved her so much that she paid little attention to his physical appearance, as he stood right in front of her, speaking and teaching. The biblical narrative leads to the deduction that she remained insensible of anything other than his godliness.

CHAPTER 17
A critical world

St. Luke's Gospel reports a visit our Lord made to the home of Martha and Mary. While Martha busily prepared food for him, her sister sat at his feet. Listening to Jesus consumed all of Mary's attention, and she had no time for busy activity. Martha's active work was good and holy, representing the first stage of the active life. Mary experienced the second stage of the active life and the first of the contemplative life. Mary concentrated on the supreme and sovereign wisdom of God cloaked by his humanity. Nothing disturbed her. She sat perfectly still at the feet of Jesus with a secret love joyfully beating upon the high *cloud of unknowing* that hovered before God.

I repeat, the only way to approach God is through this *cloud of unknowing.* Mary directed the secret yearning of her heart to this cloud. She experienced the best and holiest part of contemplation. She would not be distracted even when Martha complained to Jesus about her inactivity. Mary sat with Jesus silently, not attempting to answer Martha. She did not even frown in response to her sister's complaint. She was busy with another kind of work.

Friend, the New Testament relates this story for our benefit. Mary and Martha represent Christian contemplation and Christian activity. Mary exemplifies all contemplative personalities in every generation.

CHAPTER 18
Ignorance

In the same way that Martha complained about her sister, Mary, active persons will continue to express concern about the behavior of contemplatives. Whenever anyone turns aside from the business of the world in order to give more time to prayer and meditation, others who do not share this interest will grumble. Family and friends will speak out sharply against what they interpret as "idleness." Because they do not observe any outward activity, they assume nothing is happening. They will mention many instances (some of them true) of how other people they know about have followed the contemplative path into ruin, but will fail to mention any positive examples.

Yes, some have negative experiences while attempting a contemplative life. Dangerous risks lurk in the shadows. The devil lures away some as they seek God, because they will not listen to a reliable spiritual director. These people then become heretics and hypocrites. They fall into frenzies and other kinds of mischief, discrediting the Holy Church.

I will not digress on this issue now because I want to continue with our central topic. If it seems necessary, I may return to this subject later, giving you the reasons why such things happen.

CHAPTER 19
Complaining

Perhaps you think I am denigrating Martha, that special saint. I do not mean to dishonor her any more than I wish to speak disparagingly of those active people who do not fully comprehend and appreciate contemplatives. God forbid that you construe anything written in this book as casting scorn on any of God's servants. Martha had every right to complain that Mary was not helping her prepare lunch. When she spoke, Martha was not aware of the spiritual depth of her sister's moment with Jesus Christ. Her complaint resulted from ignorance. We may excuse her.

In the same way, we should excuse those who complain about our contemplative life, even if they speak rudely. Make allowances for their ignorance. As Martha could not perceive what occupied Mary, neither can those in the world comprehend what young disciples of God attempt when they turn away from the business of the world. If they did, they would not criticize.

I have acted and spoken inappropriately on many occasions because of ignorance. If I want God to excuse my thoughtlessness, let me be charitable and compassionate regarding the uninformed comments of others. Otherwise, I am not doing to others as I would have them do to me.

CHAPTER 20
God responds

Those attempting the contemplative life should not only excuse their critics, but also be so deeply immersed in prayer that they pay no attention to what others may say or do. Our example, Mary, conducted herself this way. Jesus will certainly do for us what he did for her.

What did he do? Notice that Martha addressed her complaint to our blessed Lord rather than to her sister. She asked him to encourage Mary to help her in the kitchen. Jesus, understanding Mary's deep immersion in contemplation, answered on her behalf. Rather than distract Mary, he spoke to Martha with gentle courtesy, defending the one fervently occupied with spiritual contemplation of God. "Martha, Martha." Speaking her name twice emphasizes the importance of response. He assured Martha that her busy work had value and importance, but that her sister engaged in a better enterprise. She was doing the one essential thing, the work of love and praising God alone. Activity and prayer mingle imperfectly, but Mary had discovered the perfect movement of love toward God. Similar in nature to heavenly bliss, divine contemplation already participates in eternity.

CHAPTER 21
The text

What does Christ mean when he says, "Mary has chosen the best part?" To designate something as "the best" implies that there is a good, a better, and a best. What then are our three options? There are not three types of lives because the church recognizes only two: active and contemplative. We may understand the story of these two sisters as an allegory describing each. No third possibility exists. We may not refer to either as "the best."

Though there are only two types of Christian living, each has three parts in varying degrees of quality. You may refer to my earlier explanation of these under the eighth heading. In the third degree of the contemplative life one experiences a dark *cloud of unknowing* where love centers privately and exclusively on God. This third stage is "the best" of all, the part Mary selected. Our Lord did not say that Mary had chosen the best manner of life, but rather that she selected the best part of two respected lives.

This best part is eternal because heaven has no need for acts of mercy. No one will be hungry or thirsty, no one will be sick or die of coldness, no one will be homeless or in jail. If God calls you to choose as Mary did, then respond wholeheartedly. Beginning here, contemplation endures forever.

The voice of Christ continues speaking to active Christians today. "Martha, Martha." We may express it this way: "Actives, actives, work hard at your merciful business now, but do not interfere with the work of contemplatives. You simply do not understand what they are doing. Leave them alone. Grant them the stillness and quiet of Mary's third and best part."

CHAPTER 22
Love and contemplation

Our Lord and Mary shared a sweet love. She greatly loved him, but he loved her even more. The account of Mary and Martha is far more than a romantic fable. Do not overlook the truth expressed in the Gospel: Mary loved Jesus so much that nothing less than his divinity could interest her. When she tearfully went to his sepulcher on Easter morning, not even angels could comfort her. They spoke to her tenderly, "Do not weep, Mary. The one you seek is risen, and you will see him again in all his beauty among his disciples in Galilee, as he promised." Even the angel's assurance was not enough to satisfy her. When we seek the king of angels, we do not settle for angels.

If you study the Scripture, you will discover other wonderful, instructive examples of this perfect love. Each narrative underscores and explains the message of this book. Study, understand, and apply them.

THOMAS À KEMPIS

From *The Imitation of Christ*

BOOK I

ADMONITIONS
USEFUL FOR A SPIRITUAL LIFE

CHAPTER 25
The Zealous Alteration of Our Lives

1. Be vigilant and diligent in the service of God, and consider often why you came here and why you have left the world.[4] Was it not so that you might live for God and become a spiritual person?

Be fervent then in your spiritual progress, for soon you will receive the reward of your labors. There will then be no more fear or sorrow for you.

You labor only a little now, and you will find great rest, even everlasting joy.

If you continue faithful and fervent in your work, without doubt God will be faithful and liberal with you in his rewards.

You must have a good hope of gaining the victory,[5] but you must not think yourself secure, for fear that you will then grow negligent or be puffed up.

2. A certain man, who often fluctuated anxiously between fear and hope, one day was oppressed with grief. Humbly he prostrated himself in a church before the altar in prayer. Within himself he said, "Oh, if only I knew that I will yet persevere to the end of my life!" All at once he heard within himself the divine answer, saying, "What would you do if you knew you would persevere? Do now what you would then, and you will be entirely secure."

Being comforted and strengthened by this, he committed himself to the will of God, and his anxious wavering ceased.

He had no desire to search curiously any further to know what should happen to him. Instead, he labored to understand what was the perfect and acceptable will of God for the beginning and accomplishing of every good work.[6]

3. "Trust in the LORD, and do good," says the psalmist, "so you will live in the land, and enjoy security."[7]

One thing deters many in their spiritual progress and fervent alteration of their lives: that is the dread of the difficulty or the cost of the conflict.

But in truth those who make the greatest effort to overcome the things that are most troublesome and repugnant to them advance the most beyond others in virtue.

We profit most and merit greater grace where we most overcome ourselves and mortify ourselves in spirit.

4. All persons do not have the same things to overcome and put to death.

But those who are diligent and fervent will be able to make greater progress than others who are of a more temperate natural disposition but less fervent in their pursuit of virtue.

Two things help us greatly to alter our lives: a violent withdrawal from the very things to which our nature is viciously inclined; and earnest labor for the good that is most lacking.

Strive also very earnestly to avoid in yourself and to overcome the faults that most frequently offend you in others.

5. Seek some spiritual profit wherever you are, and if you see or hear of any good examples, exert yourself to imitate them.

If you observe anything in others worthy of rebuke, be careful not to do the same, and if at any time you have done it, strive quickly to alter your life.

As you observe others, so also others observe you.

How good and pleasant a thing it is to see brothers and sisters fervent and devout, well mannered and well disciplined!

How sad and grievous it is to see them living in a disorderly way, not practicing that for which they are called!

How hurtful a thing it is when they neglect the good purposes of their calling, and busy themselves with things that have not been committed to them!

6. Be mindful of the profession you have made and always keep before the eyes of your mind your crucified Savior.

You have good reason to be ashamed when you look at the life of Jesus Christ, that you have not yet tried to conform to him more, even though you have long been in the way of God.

Those who will inwardly and devoutly exercise themselves in the most blessed life and passion of our Lord will find everything there that is necessary for them, so that they will have no need to seek anything beyond Jesus.

Oh, if Jesus crucified did only come into our hearts, how quickly and completely we would be taught everything necessary for us!

7. Fervent religious take and bear well all that is commanded them.

But negligent and lukewarm religious have trouble upon trouble and are afflicted on all sides, because they are without inward consolation and cannot seek outward comforts.

Religious who do not live according to their discipline open themselves up to much mischief, even to the ruin of their souls.

Those who go in search of freedom and ease will always be in anguish and sorrow, for one thing or another will always displease them.

8. Observe how religious in other communities or orders live who are under a strict monastic life.

They seldom go forth from their seclusion; they eat the poorest food, their clothing is coarse. They work much, they speak little, they have long prayer watches; they rise very early and spend much time in prayer. They read often, and discipline themselves carefully.

Consider the Carthusians, the Cistercians, and the monks and nuns of various orders, how they rise every night to sing praises to the Lord.

Therefore it would be a shame to you if you were slothful in so holy a work, when so many are beginning to praise our Lord.

9. Oh, that we had nothing else to do but always to praise the Lord with our mouth and our whole heart.

Truly if we never needed to eat or drink or sleep, but always might praise him and be mindful only of spiritual things, we would be much happier than we are now, when we are bound to serve the needs of the body.

If only there were no such needs, but only the spiritual refreshments of the soul, which—how grievous it is!—we taste too seldom.

10. When we come to such maturity that we do not go in search of consolation in any created thing, then we begin perfectly to relish God. Then we will be contented with everything that comes, whatever may happen to us.

We will then neither rejoice in having much nor be sorrowful in having little. We will entirely and confidently commit ourselves to God, who is to us all in all, to whom nothing perishes or dies, to whom all things live and at whose command they instantly serve.

11. Remember always your destination and that time lost never returns. Without care and diligence, you will never acquire virtue.

If you begin to grow lukewarm, things will begin to go poorly with you.

But if you give yourself to zeal, you will find great peace and your labors will grow lighter by the help of God's grace and your own love of virtue.

It is harder work to resist vices and passions than to toil at bodily labors.

Those who do not avoid small faults will little by little fall into greater ones.

You will always rejoice in the evening if you have spent the day well.

Be watchful over yourself, stir up yourself, admonish yourself, and regardless of what becomes of others, do not neglect yourself.

The more violence you use against your self-life, the greater will be your spiritual progress. Amen.

BOOK II

ADMONITIONS
CONCERNING THE INNER LIFE

CHAPTER 1
The Inner Life

1. "The kingdom of God is among you," says the Lord.[8] Therefore, turn with your whole heart to the Lord, forsake this wretched world, and your soul will find rest.

Learn to despise outward things and to give yourself to those that are within, and you will see the kingdom of God come within yourself.

"For the kingdom of God is . . . peace and joy in the Holy Spirit";[9] and it is not given to the wicked.

Christ will come to you and will show you his own consolations if you prepare him a worthy dwelling place in your heart.

All his glory and beauty is within,[10] and there he delights to dwell.

He often visits the inner self, and has sweet discourse with it, giving it pleasant solace, much peace, and an intimate closeness that is exceptionally wonderful.

2. Faithful soul, come then and prepare your heart for this Bridegroom, that he may grant you the special privilege of coming and dwelling within you.

For he himself says: "Those who love me will keep my word, and my Father will love them, and we will come to them and make our home with them."[11]

Give place, then, for Christ and deny entrance to all others. When you have Christ, you are rich and he alone is sufficient for you. He will be your provider and your faithful helper in every necessity, so you will not need to trust in mortal beings.

People soon change and quickly fail, but Christ abides forever and stands by us firmly to the end.[12]

3. There is no great confidence to be put in frail and mortal human beings, however helpful and dear they may be to us: nor should we be too grieved if they sometimes turn and oppose us.

Those who are on your side today may turn against you tomorrow, and often they turn like the wind.

Put your whole trust in God,[13] and let him be your love and fear above everything. He will answer for you himself and will do for you what is best.

Here we have no lasting city.[14] Wherever you may be, you are a stranger and a pilgrim, and you will never find perfect rest until you are fully united to Christ.

4. Why do you look around you here, since this is not the place of your rest? Your rest must be in heavenly things, and you must look on all earthly things as transitory and passing away.

All things pass away, and you together with them.

Beware that you do not cling to them, for fear that you may be caught up with the love of them and so perish. Let your thoughts be on the Most High, and let your prayers be directed to Christ without ceasing.

If you cannot always contemplate high and heavenly things, take rest in the passion of Christ, and willingly abide in his blessed wounds.

If you hurry devoutly toward the wounds and precious marks of Jesus, you will feel great comfort in every trouble. You will not be greatly disturbed by the humiliating discourtesies shown to you by other persons, and you will bear up easily against whatever evil words are spoken against you.

5. Christ was despised by everyone in the world, and in his greatest need was forsaken by his acquaintances and friends, and left in the midst of reproaches.[15]

He was willing to suffer wrongs and to be despised, and do you dare complain of anything?

Christ had many adversaries and backbiters; do you wish to have all other persons as your friends and benefactors?

How will your patience win its crown, if no adversity comes upon you?[16]

If you are not willing to suffer opposition, how will you be a friend of Christ?

Bear up with Christ and for Christ, if you desire to reign with Christ.

6. If only once you had entered completely into the heart of Jesus, and had tasted only a little of his ardent love, then you would not be concerned about your convenience or inconvenience, but rather would rejoice in reproaches if they come upon you, because the love of Jesus makes us despise ourselves.

Lovers of Jesus and of truth, truly inward Christians who are free from inordinate affections, can freely turn to God and rise in spirit above their self-concerns, and fruitfully rest.

7. One who views things as they are in reality, and not as they are said or thought to be, is truly wise, taught by God rather than by other persons.

One who knows how to live inwardly, to place small value on outward things, neither requires special places nor waits for proper times for performing devout exercises.

Those who live by the Spirit quickly bring their minds back to God, because they never give themselves entirely to outward things.

They are not hindered by outward labor or business, which may be necessary for the time, but as things happen, they adjust to them.

Those who are well ordered and disposed within themselves are not interested in the strange and perverse behavior of others.

We are hindered and distracted in proportion to how much we draw outward things to ourselves.

8. If your spirit were right and you were thoroughly purified from sin, all things would work out for your good and profit.[17]

The reason that many things displease and trouble you is that you are not yet completely dead to self, nor are you separated from all earthly things.

Nothing so defiles and entangles the human heart as the impure love of things created.

If you reject outward comfort, you will be able to contemplate heavenly things, and you will often be able to be filled inwardly with joy.

CHAPTER 2
Humble Submission
When We Are Corrected

1. Do not concern yourself much with who is for you and who against you, but give all your thought and care to this, that God is with you in everything you do.

Have a good conscience, and God will defend you well.

One whom God helps will never be hurt by the malice of other persons.

If you can be silent and suffer, you will surely see the help of the Lord come in your need.

He knows the time and the way to deliver you, so you ought to give yourself over to him without resistance.

God is able to help and to deliver from all confusion. It nevertheless often helps to keep us in greater humility that others know and reprimand our faults.

2. When we humble ourselves for our faults, then we easily calm others and quickly satisfy those who were angry with us.

God protects and delivers the humble.[18] The humble person he loves and comforts. He is drawn to the humble. To those who are humble he gives abundant grace; and after they have been brought low, he raises them to glory.

He reveals his secrets to the humble and tenderly draws and invites them to himself.

Although they may suffer confusion and rebuke, humble persons still have good peace, because they trust in God and not in the world.

Never think you have made any spiritual progress until you consider yourself inferior to all.

CHAPTER 3
The Peaceable Person

1. First keep yourself in peace, and then you will be able to make peace among others.

A peaceable person does more good than one who is very learned.

A passionate person turns even good to evil and easily believes the worst.

A good and peaceable person turns all things to good. Those who are in peace are not suspicious of anyone, but those who are discontented and troubled are tossed about with various suspicions. They are neither quiet themselves, nor do they allow others to be quiet.

They often speak what they should not, and omit that which they ought to have done.

They take great notice of what others should do, and neglect that which they themselves should do.[19]

So, first be fervent against yourself, and then you may justly show fervor for your neighbor's good.[20]

2. You know very well how to excuse and explain your own deeds, but you are not willing to accept the excuses of others.

It would be better to accuse yourself and excuse your neighbor.

If you want to have others bear with you, you should also bear with others.[21]

See how far you are still from true charity and humility; charitable and humble persons are not able to be angry with anyone but themselves.

It is no great thing to associate with good and gentle persons, for this is naturally pleasing to everyone, and everyone welcomes peace and loves best those who agree with them.

But to be able to live peaceably with difficult and perverse persons who lack good manners, who are willfully ignorant and undisciplined, or with those who constantly disagree with us—this is a great grace and a most commendable and masterful feat.

3. There are some who keep themselves in peace and live at peace with others.

But there are some who are not at peace in themselves and will not allow others to be in peace. They are troublesome to others, but always more troublesome to themselves.

And there are others who keep themselves in peace and seek to bring others back into peace.

Nevertheless, all our peace in this miserable life lies in humble endurance rather than in not feeling what is against us.

Those who know best how to suffer will enjoy the most peace. Such persons are conquerors of themselves, lords of the world, friends of Christ, and heirs of heaven.

CHAPTER 4
Purity and Simplicity

1. By two wings we are lifted above earthly things—simplicity and purity.

Simplicity should mark our purpose; purity our affections. Simplicity looks toward God and purity takes hold of us and tastes him.[22]

If you are free from all inordinate love, no good action will be distasteful to you.

If you intend and seek nothing but the will of God and the good of your neighbor, you will enjoy inner freedom thoroughly.

If your heart were right, then every created thing would be as a living mirror to you and a holy book of doctrine.

There is nothing created that is so small and contemptible that it does not show the goodness of God.[23]

2. If you were good and pure inwardly in your soul, you would be able to see and understand all things without hindrance and understand them correctly.

A pure heart penetrates both heaven and hell.

As we are inwardly in our hearts, so we judge outwardly.

If there is any true joy in the world, surely a person of a pure heart possesses it.

And if there is any suffering and anguish, an evil conscience knows it best.

As iron put in the fire loses its rust and becomes all red and glowing, so one who turns wholly to God puts off sluggishness and is transformed into a new person.

3. When we begin to grow lukewarm, then we are afraid of a little labor, and we gladly receive outward comforts of the world and the flesh.

But when we begin to overcome ourselves perfectly and to walk courageously in the way of God, then we regard those things lightly that before seemed so burdensome to us.

CHAPTER 5
Knowing Ourselves

1. We cannot trust much to ourselves, because we often lack grace and self-understanding.

There is only a little light in us, and even that which we have we quickly lose by negligence.

Many times we do not perceive how blind we are within.

We often do evil, and in defending it we do even worse.

Sometimes we are moved with passion and think that it is zeal.

We rebuke small faults in others, and pass over our own greater faults.

We are quick enough to feel and weigh what we suffer from others, but we think little of what others suffer from us.

Those who undertake to well and rightly weigh their own actions will not be disposed to judge others harshly.

2. Those who are truly turned to God inwardly pay attention to themselves before anything else, and those who diligently attend to their own souls easily keep silence in regard to others.

You will never be a spiritually minded and godly person unless you pass over with silence the affairs of others, and look especially to yourself.

If you attend wholly to God and yourself, what you see around you will affect you only a little.

Where are you when you are not with yourself? And when you have looked at everything and have considered at length the deeds of others, what profit is it to you if you have neglected yourself?

If you would have peace in your soul and true unity, you must put all other things aside, and attend to yourself.

3. You will make great progress if you will keep yourself free from all worldly cares.

You will lose greatly if you set great value on any temporal thing.

Let nothing be great to you, nothing high, nothing pleasing, nothing acceptable, but God himself or that which is of God.

Consider all creature comforts as vain.

A soul that loves God despises all things other than God.

God alone is eternal and of infinite greatness, filling all creation. He is the solace of the soul and the true joy of the heart.

CHAPTER 6
The Joy of a Good Conscience

1. The glory of a good person is the testimony of a good conscience.[24] Have a good conscience and you will always have joy. A good conscience can bear very much and is very cheerful in the midst of adversity.

A bad conscience is always fearful and uneasy.[25]

You will rest peacefully if your heart does not condemn you.

Never rejoice unless you have done well.

Wicked persons never know true joy nor feel inward peace, because "There is no peace for the wicked," says the Lord.[26]

And if they should say, "We are in peace, no evil will happen to us,[27] and who will dare hurt us?" do not believe them; for all of a sudden the wrath of God will arise, their deeds will come to nothing, and their thoughts will perish.[28]

2. To glory in suffering is not a hard thing for one who truly loves God; for to glory in this way is to glory in the cross of our Lord Jesus Christ.

The glory given and received by mortals is fleeting and short-lived.

The glory of this world is always accompanied by sorrow.

The glory of good persons is in their consciences, not in the tongues of others. The gladness of righteous persons is in God and from God, and their joy is in the truth.

Those who desire true and everlasting glory do not value the glory of the world.

And those who go in search of temporal glory, or who do not despise it from their souls, show that they have only a little love for the glory of heaven.

They enjoy great tranquility of heart who care neither for the praise nor the condemnation of others.

3. They will easily be peaceful and content whose consciences are clean.

You are no more holy if you are praised, or worse if you are rebuked.

What you are, you are, and words cannot make you greater than you are in the eyes of God.

If you consider well what you are within yourself, you will not care what others say about you outwardly.

Humans look on the outward appearance, but God looks on the heart.[29] Humans consider the deeds, but God weighs the motives.

To be always doing well and to think that you have done only a little is the sign of the humble soul.

To be unwilling to have any created being for our comfort is a sign of great purity and inward trust.

4. Those who go in search of no testimony on their behalf from the outside, show that they have wholly committed themselves to God.

"For it is not those who commend themselves that are approved," says St. Paul, "but those whom the Lord commends."[30]

To walk inwardly with God, and not to be held by any outward affections, is the state of a spiritual person.

CHAPTER 7
Loving Jesus Above All Things

1. Blessed are those who know how good it is to love Jesus, and to despise themselves for the sake of Jesus.

They must give up every other love for this Beloved, for Jesus desires to be loved alone above all things.

The love of created things is deceitful and unstable, but the love of Jesus is faithful and abiding.

Those who cling to created things will fall with them. Those who embrace Jesus will stand firm in him forever.

Love him, and hold him as your friend, for he will not forsake you when all others leave you, nor allow you to perish in the end.

One day you will have to be separated from everyone, whether you want to or not.

2. Therefore, living or dying, keep close to Jesus and commit yourself to his faithfulness. He alone can help you when everything else fails you.

Your Beloved is of such a nature that he will allow no rival, but desires to have your heart's love for himself only, and desires to reign there on his own throne.

If you would learn to empty yourself of all created things, Jesus would readily dwell with you.

Whatever trust you put in people, apart from Jesus, will be little better than wasted.

Do not trust or lean on a reed shaken by the wind, for all people are grass and all their glory will fade and wither as the flower of the field.[31]

3. If you look only on the outward appearance of people, you will soon be deceived.

For if you seek comfort and gain in others, you will feel great spiritual loss because of it.

If you seek Jesus in all things, you will surely find Jesus.

If you seek yourself, you will find yourself indeed, but to your own great loss.

For truly we are more hurtful to ourselves, if we do not seek Jesus, than all the world and all our enemies.

CHAPTER 8
The Intimate Friendship of Jesus

1. When Jesus is present, all is well and nothing seems difficult; but when Jesus is absent, everything is hard.

When Jesus does not speak inwardly to us, all other comfort is worth nothing; but if Jesus speaks just one word, we feel great consolation.

Did not Mary arise immediately from her weeping when Martha said to her, "The Teacher is here and is calling for you"?[32]

Happy is the moment when Jesus calls us from tears to joy of spirit.

How parched and hard-hearted you are without Jesus! How foolish and vain if you desire anything beyond Jesus!

Is not this a greater loss to you than if you were to lose the whole world?[33]

2. What can the world confer on you without Jesus? To be without Jesus is the gravest hell; and to be with Jesus is a sweet paradise.

If Jesus is with you, no enemy can grieve or hurt you.[34]

Whoever finds Jesus finds a good treasure, yes, a good that is above all good.[35]

And those who lose Jesus lose very much, yes, more than all the world.

They are most poor who live without Jesus; and they are most rich who are dear to Jesus.[36]

3. It is a great art to know how to live with Jesus, and to know how to hold on to Jesus is great wisdom.

Be humble and peaceable, and Jesus will be with you.[37]

Be devout and quiet, and Jesus will remain with you.

You may quickly drive Jesus away and lose his favor if you turn back to outward things.

And if you drive him from you and lose him, to whom will you turn, and what friend will you seek then?

Without a friend you cannot live well, and if Jesus is not your friend above all, you will be extremely sad and desolate.

Therefore you act very foolishly if you put your trust or begin to rejoice in any other.[38]

It is better to have the entire world against us than to have Jesus be offended with us.

Of all therefore that are dear and beloved to you, let Jesus alone be the most beloved.

4. Let all be loved for Jesus' sake, but Jesus for his own sake.

Jesus Christ alone is to be loved exclusively, because he alone is found to be good and faithful before all other friends.

In him and for him let friends and foes be dear to you. All these are to be prayed for, that all may know and love him.[39]

Never desire to be the object of praise or love above others, for that belongs only to God, who has none like himself.

Do not desire that anyone's heart be set on you, and do not set your heart on the love of anyone, but let Jesus be in you and in every good person.

5. Be pure and free inwardly, and do not become entangled by any created thing.

You should be devoid of concealment and open before God, ever carrying a pure heart toward him, if you want to know rest and feel how sweet the Lord is.

And truly, unless you are preceded and drawn by his grace, you will never attain to that happiness of forsaking and leaving all in order to be inwardly knit and united to him.

For when the grace of God comes to us, then we are enabled to do all things, and when it departs, we are weak and poor, and, so to speak, given up to afflictions.

In this case, you should not be downcast or despairing, but should resign yourself calmly to the will of God, to bear whatever comes upon you for the glory of Jesus Christ; for summer follows winter; after the night, day returns; and after the storm, there comes a great calm.

CHAPTER 9
The Lack of Comfort

1. It is not hard to despise human comfort when we have the comfort that is divine.

It is a great thing indeed to be able to bear the loss of both human and divine comfort, and, for God's honor, to be willing to endure this desolation of heart, to seek ourselves in nothing, and not to look to our own merit.

What great thing is it to be cheerful and devout when grace comes to you? That is a time desired by everyone.

It is pleasant to ride when we are carried by the grace of God.

And what wonder is it if we do not feel our burden when we are borne up by the Almighty and led by the Sovereign Guide?

2. We gladly hold on to anything for solace and comfort, and it is difficult to cast off the false love of self.

The blessed martyr St. Lawrence, through the love of God, mightily overcame the love of the world and of himself, despising what seemed delightful in the world. For the love of Christ he patiently suffered when Pope Sixtus, whom he dearly loved, was taken from him.[40]

He therefore overcame loving other persons by loving the Creator, choosing what pleased God rather than human comfort.

So also, you must learn to give up even a near and dear friend for the love of God.

And do not think it is hard when a friend forsakes you, since you know that we must all at the last be separated from one another.

3. We must strive long and mightily with ourselves before we can learn fully to master ourselves and turn our whole affection toward God.

When we put trust in ourselves, we easily come to depend on human comforts.

But one who truly loves Christ and is a diligent seeker of virtue does not lean on these comforts or seek such perceptible sweetness, but chooses rather hard trials and heavy labors for Christ.

When God therefore gives you spiritual comfort, receive it with thankfulness; but know that it is a gift of God, not your deserving.

4. Do not be proud, or take too much joy in spiritual comfort, or be vainly presumptuous. Rather be more humble on account of the gift, more careful and cautious in your actions; for the time of comfort will pass away and temptation will follow.

When consolation is removed from you, do not immediately despair, but wait in humility and patience for the heavenly visitation; for God is able to give back again more ample consolation.

This is nothing new or strange to those who have experience in the ways of God; for the great saints and ancient prophets often experienced such changes.

5. One said at the time when grace was with him, "I said in my prosperity, 'I shall never be moved.'"[41]

But afterward, when grace was withdrawn, he said, "You hid your face from me, and I was dismayed."

Yet in the meantime he did not despair, but sought the Lord more earnestly, saying, "To you, O Lord, I cried, and to the Lord I made supplication."

At length he received the fruit of his prayer and testified that he was heard, saying, "The Lord heard me and had mercy on me; the Lord became my helper."

But how? "You have turned my sorrow into joy," he said, "and you have clothed me with gladness."

If great saints were dealt with in this way, we who are weak and poor should not despair if we sometimes grow hot or cold; for the Spirit comes and goes according to the good pleasure of his own will.[42] It was for this cause that blessed Job says, "You visit them every morning and test them at every moment."[43]

6. On what then can I hope, or in what can I trust, but only in the great mercy of God and only in hope of heavenly grace?

For whether I have with me good persons, devout brothers and sisters, or faithful friends; whether I have holy books, fine treatises, or sweet hymns and songs—all these help only a little and are of little comfort when I am deprived of grace and left in my own poverty.

At such a time there is no better remedy than patience and the denial of myself according to the will of God.[44]

7. I have never found anyone so spiritual and devout as not to experience at times a withdrawal of grace or to feel some decrease of fervor.

There was never a saint who was so highly transported with love or illuminated, who sooner or later was not tempted.

For no one is worthy of the high gift of the contemplation of God who has not been exercised by some trying experience for God's sake.

For, temptation going before is often the sign of consolation to follow.

To those who have been tested by temptations, heavenly comfort is promised. Therefore God says, "To everyone who conquers, I will give permission to eat from the tree of life."[45]

8. Divine consolation is given to us so that we may be stronger when adversities come.

But temptation follows so that we may not be puffed up in pride by such benefit.

The devil does not sleep, neither is the flesh as yet dead: therefore you must prepare yourself for battle, for you have enemies on the right and on the left, who never rest.

CHAPTER 10
Gratitude for the Grace of God

1. Why do you seek rest, since you were born to labor? Prepare yourself for patience rather than consolations, to bear the Cross rather than to rejoice.

What worldly persons are there who would not gladly receive spiritual comfort and joy if they could always have it?

For spiritual comforts exceed all the delights of the world and the pleasures of the flesh.

For all worldly delights are either vain or unclean, while spiritual delights alone are pleasant and honest, springing from virtues and poured forth by God into pure minds.

But such divine consolations none of us can have as we would like, for the time of temptation is never far away.

2. A false liberty of mind and a great confidence in self are very opposite to heavenly visitations.

God does well in giving the grace of consolation, but we do evil in not returning it all again to him with thanksgiving.

Therefore the gifts of grace cannot flow in us, because we are ungrateful to the Giver, and do not return them wholly to the Fountain from whom all good comes.[46]

Grace is always given to those who are ready to yield thanks for grace received, but from the proud is taken what is freely given to the humble.

3. I do not desire any consolation that takes away any sting of conscience, nor any contemplation that leads to pride.

For all that is high is not holy, nor is all that is sweet good, nor is every desire pure; neither is everything that is dear to us pleasing to God.

I willingly accept that grace whereby I may be made humbler, more careful, and more ready to renounce myself.

Those who are taught by the gift of grace and schooled by its withdrawals, will not dare to think that any goodness comes from themselves, but will openly confess that they are poor and defenseless.

Give to God what is God's[47] and ascribe to yourself what is yours: that is, give thanks to God for his grace, and acknowledge that to yourself alone belong your fault and the fitting punishment of the fault.

4. Always put yourself in the lowest place and the highest will be given you; for the highest cannot stand without the lowest.

The greatest saints before God are least in their own judgments, and the more glorious they are, the more humble within themselves they are.

Those who are full of truth and the glory of heaven are not desirous of vain display.

Those who are firmly settled and grounded in God can in no way be proud.

Those who ascribe to God whatever good they have received do not seek glory from one another, but the glory that comes from God alone. Desiring above all things that God may be praised in themselves and in all his saints, they constantly press on for this very thing.

Be thankful for even the smallest thing and you will be worthy to receive greater things.

Let the least be to you as greatest, and the most contemptible as a special gift.

If you consider the dignity of the Giver, no gift will seem little or too contemptible to value. For that which is given by the Most High God cannot be small.

Yes, even though God may give punishment and blows with a rod, it ought to be acceptable, because whatever he permits to happen to us is always for our salvation.

Let those who desire to retain the favor of God be thankful for grace given, and let them be patient when it is taken away. Let them pray that grace may return; let them be careful and humble in spirit, so that they do not lose it.

CHAPTER 11
How Few Are the Lovers of the Cross of Jesus

1. Jesus has many lovers of his heavenly kingdom, but few bearers of his cross.

He has many seekers of consolation, but few of suffering.

He finds many companions at his feasting, but few at his fasting.

All desire to rejoice with him; few are willing to endure anything for him.

Many follow Jesus as far as the breaking of bread, but few to the drinking of the cup of his passion.[48]

Many reverence his miracles, but few will follow the shame of his cross.

Many love Jesus as long as no adversities come upon them.

Many praise and bless him as long as they receive some consolation from him.

But if Jesus hides himself and leaves them only for a brief time, they begin to complain or become overly despondent in mind.

2. Those who love Jesus for Jesus' sake, and not for any comforts they receive, bless him as readily in temptation and anguish of heart as in the state of highest consolation.

And though he may never send them consolation, yet they desire always to praise him and give him thanks.

3. What power there is in pure love of Jesus when it is not mixed with self-interest and self-love!

Are not they to be called hirelings—serving for purely mercenary motives—who are always looking for consolations?

Do they not show by their actions that they are lovers of self rather than of Christ, who are always thinking of their own advantage and profit?[49]

Where can even one person be found who is willing to serve God for nothing?

4. Rarely is there anyone who is so spiritual as to be thoroughly free from leaning on created things. The worth of such a person is beyond calculation!

If we should give all we own, yet it is nothing. And if we practice great penance, still it is little. And though we may understand all knowledge, we are still far off.

And if we should have great virtue and be fervent in devotion, even there is still much lacking, especially the one thing most necessary for us.

What is that? That forsaking all, we forsake ourselves, go completely away from ourselves, and keep nothing of self-love.[50]

And having done all things that we know to be our duty, let us think that we have done nothing.

5. Let us not think that to be great which others esteem great, but let us in truth confess ourselves to be unprofitable servants, as the Truth himself says, "When you have done all things commanded you, say, 'We are unworthy servants.' "[51] Then we may well be called poor in spirit, and we may well say with the prophet, "I am lonely and afflicted."[52]

Yet there is no one richer, no one freer, no one more powerful than we are, for we know how to forsake ourselves and all things, and truly put ourselves in the lowest place.

CHAPTER 12
The Royal Way of the Holy Cross

1. This seems to many to be a hard saying: "If any want to become my followers, let them deny themselves and take up their cross and follow me."[53]

But it will be much harder to hear these words at the last day: "You that are accursed, depart from me into the eternal fire."[54]

For those who now gladly and willingly hear and follow the word of the cross will not then be afraid that they will hear the sentence of everlasting damnation.

This sign of the cross will appear in heaven when the Lord comes to judgment.

Then all the servants of the cross, who in their lifetime conformed themselves to the Crucified One, will draw near to Christ the Judge with great boldness.

2. Why do you dread to take up the cross, since it is the very way to the kingdom of heaven?

In the cross is salvation; in the cross is life; in the cross is defense against our enemies; in the cross is infusion of heavenly sweetness; in the cross is strength of mind; in the cross is joy of spirit; in the cross is the height of virtue; in the cross is the perfection of holiness.

There is no health of the soul or hope of eternal life, other than in the cross.

Take up your cross, therefore, and follow Jesus, and you will go into everlasting life. He went before you bearing his own cross[53] and died for you upon the cross, so that you might also bear your cross and that you should be ready to die on the cross.

For if you die with him, you will also live with him. And if you share his suffering, you will also share his glory.[56]

3. See then how everything hangs on the cross, and how everything depends on dying on it. There is no other way to life and true inward peace, except the way of the holy cross and of daily self-denial.

Go where you will, seek whatever you will, you will not find a higher way above or a safer way below, than the way of the holy cross.

Dispose everything according to your will and judgment, yet you will still find that you will of necessity have something to suffer, willingly or unwillingly, and so you will always find the cross.

For either you will feel pain in your body or in soul or suffer trouble of spirit.

4. You will sometimes feel forsaken by God, at other times you will be troubled by your neighbors, and what is more, you will sometimes be a burden to yourself.

Yet you cannot find remedy or comfort for your trouble as long as God wills you to bear it.

For God would have you learn to suffer trying experiences without consolation, so that you will submit yourself wholly to him and to become more humble by suffering.

No one feels the suffering of Jesus so intensely as one who has suffered similar things.

The cross is always ready, therefore, and waits for you everywhere.

You cannot escape it wherever you run; for wherever you may go, you take yourself with you, and you will always find yourself.

Turn upward, turn downward, turn outward, turn inward, you will find the cross everywhere, so you always need patience if you would have inward peace and win a lasting crown.

5. If you bear the cross cheerfully, it will bear you and bring you to your desired goal, where there will be an end of suffering, even though this cannot be here.

If you bear the cross unwillingly, you make a great burden for yourself and greatly increase your load, though you will still have to bear it.

If you cast away one cross, you will undoubtedly find another, and that perhaps a heavier one.

6. Do you think you can escape what no other human has been able to avoid? Which of the saints was without the cross and trials in this world?

For not even our Lord Jesus Christ was ever one hour without some sorrow and pain as long as he lived here. "It was necessary," he says, "that the Christ should suffer and rise again from the dead and then enter into his glory."[57] And how is it then that you seek another way than this royal way, which is the way of the holy cross?

7. The whole life of Christ was cross and martyrdom, and do you seek pleasure and joy for yourself?

You are wrong, you are wrong if you seek anything other than to suffer trials; for this whole mortal life is full of miseries and is marked on every side with crosses.

The further we advance in spirit, so much heavier are the crosses we often find, because the pain of our exile increases with our love.

8. Nevertheless we who are afflicted in so many ways, are not without some comfort, for we see well that great fruit and benefit will be ours by the bearing of our own cross.

For while we willingly submit ourselves to such trial, then all the burden of suffering is turned into assurance of divine consolation.

And the more the flesh is subdued by affliction, the more the spirit is strengthened by inward grace.

And sometimes it feels such comfort in adversities, that for desire to be conformed to the cross of Christ, it would not want to be without sorrow and affliction;[58] for it believes that the more it bears for him here, the more acceptable it will be to God.

It is not a person's virtue, but the grace of God that enables a frail human to attempt and love that which by nature we abhor and fear.

9. It is not our way to bear the cross, to love the cross, to discipline the body and bring it into subjection to the spirit, to flee honors, to suffer being insulted, to despise ourselves and to want to be despised, to endure all adversities and losses, and to desire no prosperity in this world.

If you trust in yourself, you will never be able to bring this about.

But if you trust in the Lord, strength will be given you from heaven, and the world and the flesh will be made subject to your command.

If you are armed with faith and signed with the cross of Christ, you will not fear your enemy the devil.

10. Set yourself, then, like a good and faithful servant of Christ to bear courageously the cross of your Lord, who out of love for you was crucified.

Prepare yourself to bear many adversities and various kinds of troubles in this miserable life; for so it will be with you wherever you may be, or wherever you may hide yourself.

It must be so, and there is no remedy or way of escape from the trying experience of evils and sorrows, but to bear them patiently.

Drink lovingly of the cup of the Lord if you desire to be his friend and to have a share with him.[59]

As for consolations, leave them to God to do as will best please him.

But prepare yourself to bear trying experiences and account them the greatest comforts; for "the sufferings of this present time are not worth comparing with the glory about to be revealed to us,"[60] even if you alone could suffer them all.

11. When you come to this, that trying experiences are sweet and pleasant to you for Christ's sake, then you consider that it is well with you, for you have found paradise on earth.

As long as suffering is grievous to you and you long to escape, so long will you suffer trouble, and trying experiences will follow you everywhere.

12. If you set yourself to that condition in which you should be, that is to suffer gladly for God and to die fully to the world, then it will quickly be better with you and you will find peace.

Even if you, like St. Paul, were "caught up into the third heaven," you would not then be free from all adversity. For Jesus says, "I myself will show him how much he must suffer for the sake of my name."[61]

Suffering, therefore, awaits you if you desire to love Jesus and constantly serve him.

13. Would to God you were worthy to suffer something for the name of Jesus![62] How great a glory would await you! What gladness among all the saints of God! How edified would be those around you!

For all persons praise patience, but few are willing to suffer.

How right it is to be willing to suffer some little thing for Christ's sake, since many suffer much more grievous things for the world.

14. Know this for certain, you must lead a dying life. The more you die to yourself, the more you begin to live to God.

None of us is fit to receive the understanding of heavenly things if we have not submitted ourselves to bear adversities for Christ.

Nothing is more acceptable to God, nothing more profitable to you in this world than to suffer cheerfully for Christ.

And if you had to choose, you should rather choose adversity for Christ than to be refreshed by a multitude of consolations, because in this way you would be more like Christ and his saints.

For our merit and our spiritual advancement does not consist in comforts and sweetness, but in bearing great adversities and trying experiences.

15. For surely if there had been anything better and more useful than suffering for the health of the human soul, Christ would certainly have shown it by word and example.

But he openly exhorts the disciples who follow him and all others who desire to follow him to bear the cross, saying, "If any want to become my followers, let them deny themselves and take up their cross and follow me."[63]

So, all things searched and read, this is the final conclusion, that through much distress and suffering resulting from persecution we must enter the kingdom of God.[64]

BRIEF BIOGRAPHIES
OF THE CONTRIBUTORS

SAINT AUGUSTINE
354–430

Augustine stands as one of the greatest and most influential of Christian theologians. "It may be safely predicted, that while the mind of man yearns for knowledge, and his heart seeks rest, the *Confessions* will retain that foremost place in the world's literature which it has secured by its sublime outpourings of devotion and profound philosophical spirit."[65]

It should be borne in mind that the *Confessions* was not intended to be an intellectual exercise, removed from the everyday realities of life. In it, Augustine seeks to lay bare his heart, his soul—before God and before his fellow men. It is an honest book and a book that speaks to the heart first of all.

We moderns may find some difficulty in his allegorizations, especially those found in the last three books. But one translator aptly remarked, "Where the strict use of history is not disregarded, (to use Augustine's expression), allegorizing, by way of spiritual meditation, may be profitable." Certainly his insights are not to be despised!

Born in 352, in the small city of Tagaste, Africa (in what is now Algeria), Augustine lived in the time of the growing ascendancy of the Christian Church and the growing decline of the Roman empire. It was scarcely a quarter of a century earlier that the great Council of Nicaea had been held, and there were heresies and schisms throughout the Christian world that still held sway over hearts and minds. Donatists continued to hold that many Catholic orders were invalid because they came through *traditori* (those who had denied the faith during the severe persecution and had later repented and been restored to the Church). In his later years Augustine would spend much effort in fighting for the unity of the Church against their schismatic beliefs. Arianism (denying the full divinity of Christ) succeeded in winning the allegiance of the Emperor and his mother, and echoes of that threat to the peace and unity of the Church continued to resound throughout Augustine's lifetime. But for Augustine personally, his sojourn among the Manicheans gave the background for much of the material we find in the *Confessions*. After his schooling under a harsh tutor in Tagaste, he was sent to Madaura for a time. Family finances forced his return home and resulted in an idle year, 369–70. He was then sent to Carthage, to what would be equivalent to a university, where he distinguished himself in the rhetorical school. His father died in 371, but his mother continued to support his schooling with the aid of a wealthy patron, Romanianus. It is evident that she continued to cherish high ambitions for his worldly success. While at Carthage, Augustine came under the influence of the Manicheans and took a mistress, to whom he was faithful for fifteen years. To them was born one son, Adeodatus.

After some years of teaching at Carthage, Augustine decided to go to Rome. His mother opposed the idea, but could not dissuade him. After a brief stay in Rome, he was appointed in 385 as Public Teacher of Rhetoric at Milan, where he first came under the influence of St. Ambrose. In 385–86, the Empress Justina demanded the surrender of two churches to the Arians. Ambrose led his people in a refusal to surrender the churches, even when confronted by military force. Augustine was aware of this crisis, but he was not personally involved.

Ten years spent with the Manicheans had brought Augustine many intellectual difficulties with their system. Although they had encouraged his own skeptical approach to the Holy Scriptures, they had not satisfied his thirst for sure knowledge nor his growing uneasiness with his disorderly life. With his mother's help, Augustine's mistress was dismissed and arrangements were made for his marriage, which had to be postponed because his intended was underage. But his struggles with the flesh resulted in his taking a new mistress, because he felt morally incapable of making a better choice. He chronicles the inner struggles which led, with timely help from Ambrose, to his departure from the Manicheans and his conversion to the Catholic faith. He was baptized at Easter, 387, along with his son, Adeodatus. Having resigned his position as professor of rhetoric, he and his company were waiting for a ship to make their way back to Africa when his mother suddenly became ill and died at Ostia, the port of Rome.

The next year, having returned to Tagaste and sold his property there, Augustine set up a monastic kind of community with a few friends, continuing his writing. In 391, with much misgiving on his part, he consented to be ordained presbyter at Hippo, a nearby city of about 30,000. The Church was not strong there, the city's population being a mixture of pagans, Jews, several schismatic sects, and a large group of Donatists. In 395 (in violation of the eighth canon of Nicaea) he was made assistant bishop to the aged Valerius, and succeeded him as bishop the following year.

It was not long after his election as bishop that he began the *Confessions*, completing them probably in 398. Thus they represent his thought and the account of his life in its midstream.

144 Praying with Your Whole Heart

He wrote this book "at the request of friends who begged him to commit to writing those recollections of his former life to which he often referred in private conversation. He consented for the characteristic reason that he desired his friends to mourn and rejoice along with him as they followed his retrospect of past years, and on his behalf to give thanks to God."[66]

Augustine's years as bishop involved struggles with errors he believed to be a threat to salvation and to the welfare of the Church on several fronts: Manicheans, Donatists, Arians, and Pelagians. In addition to these very real battles, the Roman Empire itself was under mortal assault. It is one of the great ironies of history that as Augustine finished his immortal *City of God* in the quiet of his monastic residence, the Vandals were pillaging the countryside of North Africa. "While the Vandals besieged Hippo, St. Augustine died (August 28, 410) in the sanctity and poverty in which he had lived for many years. Shortly afterward, the Vandals destroyed the city, but left his cathedral and library untouched."[67]

Sending the *Confessions* to a friend, Augustine wrote, "In these behold me, that you may not praise me beyond what I am. Believe what is said of me, not by others, but by myself."[68]

SAINT CATHERINE OF SIENA
1347–1380

Biographers of Catherine have faced great difficulties in reconstructing the life of their subject, because her life is so embedded in legend and piety. In addition, some of the earliest biographies of Catherine were themselves hagiographies, creating a portrait of a pious mystical woman whose transports to God made her an unreachable subject. Even so, there are many facets of Catherine's life of which we can be sure.

Catherine was born in 1347 to a wool dyer in the Fontebranda district of Siena. Caterina di Giacomo di Benincasa, a precocious young girl, was the twenty-fourth of twenty-five children. She was a headstrong and independent child, clever and ingenious in her religious devotion. Catherine's passionate desire for truth and the knowledge of God motivated her very being, even in her youth.

The Dominican Order influenced Catherine greatly. She often visited the church and cloister of San Domenico, a hub of Dominican teaching, spending a great deal of time with these teachers. She was also influenced in Dominican teachings by the brother of her brother-in-law Tommaso della Fonte, who had joined the Dominican order in 1349.

Another group that impressed Catherine was a group of women in Siena known as the *Mantellate*. These women, who wore the habit of the Dominican Order, lived in their homes and ministered to the sick and poor. Even though they did not live in a cloister, they were directed by a prioress. By the time she was fourteen, Catherine had decided not to marry, and she sought and gained entrance to this group of women.

Raymond Capua, her earliest biographer and close friend, records that Catherine vowed her virginity to God when she was just seven years old. At fifteen, she defied her parents and refused their efforts to force her to marry, and at eighteen she obtained the Dominican habit. After she joined the Dominicans, she lived for a period of about three years in silence and solitude, leaving her room only to attend Mass. By the time she was twenty-one, she had experienced her "mystical espousal" to Christ. Soon after she began her work with the Mantellate.

Much like Mother Teresa, Catherine devoted herself to taking care of the sick and indigent. However, during this period of ministering to society, she never gave up her contemplative life, and could often be found at home in her room teaching her followers about the Bible, theology, and God's grace and truth.

In 1370, Catherine had one of her most profound mystical experiences—her "mystical death." For four hours she experienced ecstatic union with God, even though to outside observers she appeared to be dead. This experience led her to become more severe in her self-discipline, and enabled her to have a clear vision of the ways that she could introduce God's truth to the world.

From the time of her "mystical death" to her physical death, Catherine worked tirelessly in political and religious affairs. In 1375, in Pisa, she preached that military strength could be best used to win unbelievers in the Holy Land. She preached that shedding one's blood for Christ was an honorable mission, and so she supported a Crusade through her words. In the same year she received the stigmata, though by her own request these wounds were not visible.

Catherine soon became involved in urging Gregory XI to move the papacy from Avignon back to Rome. During these years she was also active in preaching about clergy reform and martyrdom through Crusades. After Gregory's death, Urban VI replaced him as pope. Because many people opposed Urban when he was elected pope, Catherine foresaw the possibility that schism could occur in the Church. She began a furious letter-writing campaign in order to urge fidelity to the Church. Much of this urging makes its way into her book, *The Dialogue*.

Sometime between 1375 and 1378, Catherine founded a women's monastery outside of Siena in the old fortress of Belcaro. During these years she wrote *The Dialogue*. In this, her most famous writing, she expressed many of her concerns about Church unity, personal austerity and devotion, love of neighbor, clergy reform, God's grace and mercy, and the passionate search for God's truth.

From the time Catherine was thirty until her death at thirty-three, she directed a "household" in Siena where women and men lived by strict observance to poverty and alms. Her final years were filled with physical agony, even though she managed to attend services at Saint Peter's each day. She died on April 29, 1380, and since 1969, the Roman Catholic Church has observed April 29 as her feast day.

THE ANONYMOUS AUTHOR
OF *THE CLOUD OF UNKNOWING*,
FOURTEENTH CENTURY

I f you are serious about your prayer life, this book is for you. The writer offers helpful spiritual instruction for those who are learning to pray, guiding them logically and clearly toward ideal prayer—what he calls "perfect" prayer. This anonymous fourteenth-century author of *The Cloud of Unknowing* originally prepared this book for cloistered English monks. A keen observer of human behavior, he laughed down the violations of good common sense that he saw religious communities employing.

Though scholars have struggled for centuries to discover the writer's identity and to place him in a particular religious order, the humble guide stubbornly remains unknown.

He is not interested in telling us how profound his own prayer life is, though we can clearly see that it is substantial. Instead, his intent is to extend a helping hand to the rest of us. He communicates, as Jesus did in the Gospels, with ordinary, everyday language. No doubt he would have been astonished to discover how many would find his little book a key spiritual guide down through the centuries.

In his time, England and much of Europe were immersed in mystical religions. Practitioners of necromancy and sorcery experimented widely. The whole culture was intensely religious. Into this context Christian mystics, addressing the devout life, introduced a healthier spiritual tone and wrote what were to become timeless works. Meister Eckhart, Henry Suso, John Tauler, Walter Hilton, Julian of Norwich, Richard

Rolle, Catherine of Siena, Thomas à Kempis, and others wrote during this period.

The fourteenth century was also a time of social, artistic, and political revolution. The unknown writer of *The Cloud* gives that century and following centuries something genuine, something worth our aspiration. He does so with a smile on his face and a twinkle in his eye. He is attractive to readers in the way that Jesus Christ is attractive: he is serious without being stuffy. He talks about important religious issues, but he does so without becoming haughty.

The anonymous author is intelligent, but he avoids and criticizes convoluted academic style. A master of hyperbole, he employs colorful language to emphasize the spiritual hazards of formal education. He does not come across as anti-intellectual, but simply observes that theological erudition offers little service to one's prayer life. What we find in these pages is a healthy mysticism simply based in growing toward God. It is not a book of spiritual tricks that lead to a quick jolt of spiritual fireworks, but offer little for the remaining journey.

The Cloud of Unknowing contains seventy-five chapters (*chapitres*). For such a slim book, that equals about one chapter per page. While they may seem more like section breaks than new chapters, they are markers along the way of sustained and developing thought. Although he briefly digresses a time or two, he otherwise sticks tenaciously to his subject, and at the end of the book he returns the reader to the place he began.

The author sometimes struggles to express himself clearly, fearing that his readers will only take his words at face value. He knows that if readers do not keep in mind the overall direction of the book, they may wind up in seemingly contradictory theological dead ends. For example, when the writer mentions that the idea of God, being spirit, is more compatible with a purely spiritual desire (one not based on emotional human desires), some may read that and come to an erroneous conclusion. Rather than leading the reader into a trap, he points out that the purer our spirituality, the more it is in harmony with God's spirit.

Some modern readers may have difficulty with the concept of the devil, or Satan, who is often mentioned in *The Cloud of Unknowing*. The author attributes many religious mistakes to the devil's work. We have included these passages as the author originally expressed them. As you read these sections, remind yourself that religious thought in this period of our history includes the active influence of a personal devil. In Wartburg Castle, where Martin Luther worked on his translation of the Bible, tourists are shown a spot on the wall where Luther threw an inkbottle at the devil in 1521. His hymn "A Mighty Fortress Is Our God" assures us that devils, who threaten to undo us, fill our world:

> *For still our ancient foe*
> *Doth seek to work us woe;*
> *His craft and power are great;*
> *And, armed with cruel hate,*
> *On earth is not his equal.*

Thomas Aquinas, in *Summa Theologiae*, writing in the thirteenth century, points out that Holy Scripture describes the properties of intelligible things with natural images.

Following Aquinas, the anonymous author contends that angels and demons can take on the bodily appearance congruent with the content of their business among us.

Repetition of ideas is characteristic of the classical writing style of the period. While this may help to drive a point into memory, it seems like wheel-spinning to modern readers. Our anonymous author avoids this hazard. *The Cloud of Unknowing*, already a brief book, does not cry out for condensation, as do other spiritual classics.

THOMAS À KEMPIS
CA. 1380–1471

Thomas Hammerken was born in 1380 in Kempin, a small, walled town near Cologne, Germany. His brother John, fifteen years his senior, went early into the religious life. When Thomas was twelve, he went at his brother's advice to Deventer, where Florentius received him and provided schooling, housing, books, and board for the next seven years. He attended the village school, run by the brothers, sang in the choir, and "learned to write," joining the noble copyists at their work.

After his training at Deventer, Thomas went in 1399, with Florentius's blessing, to Mount St. Agnes, the first daughterhouse of Windesheim, where his brother John had been cofounder and was now prior. Florentius sent a request that the rule against having two brothers in the same monastery be set aside in their case, and it was done. Here Thomas spent the rest of his long life. He waited six years before becoming a novice, and on June 10, 1406, he made his solemn profession as an Augustinian Canon Regular. Seven more years would pass before he was ordained, at the age of thirty-three.

Once we hear of his traveling to Windesheim on business. In 1429 he accompanied the rest of the brethren in their migration to Ludenkerk, to avoid the papal interdict that Windesheim suffered as a result of a disputed canonical election. During this absence, Thomas was called away from Ludenkerk to the Convent of Bethany, to care for his dying brother John. Altogether he was away from Mount St. Agnes for about three years out of seventy-two. Twice he was elected sub-prior and once he was procurator (or bursar) of the community. But he was not a good business manager, and he appears to have been glad to return to literary work, training the novices, and meditating in his beloved cell.

It had been the practice of Gerard Groote and Florentius to encourage the brothers to keep a book of extracts from their readings—pithy and meaningful sayings and thoughts gleaned mainly from their reading. Gerard set the example himself, and has, indeed, been credited by some as being the real author of this book. Without doubt, his practice of encouraging the keeping of *raparia,* as these books were called, lies behind the book. Since the *raparia* were kept for the good of all, Thomas would have had access not only to his own book, but also to those of others, greatly expanding the numbers of authors who would become known to him. It is not surprising, therefore, that we find allusions or quotations from St. Augustine, St. Bernard of Clairvaux, St. Francis of Assisi, St. Thomas Aquinas, St. Bonaventura, St. Gregory the Great, and even from such classical authors as Aristotle, Ovid, and Seneca. There are also echoes of medieval Latin hymns, and "you can scarcely read a sentence," said one observer, "that does not recall some passage, now in the Old, now in the New Testament."

Apart from his historical sources, even remembrances that the author quotes unconsciously, there is the stamp of immediate inspiration and the spark of fire of a soul that is turned to God and is listening to what the Spirit is saying. When he says, "I will hear what the Lord God will speak in me" (Book III, Chapter 1), we can believe that he means exactly that, and that he is listening in spirit to the inner voice of the Consoler and Strengthener of Christians, the Holy Spirit.

From many references in the *Imitation,* it is obvious that Thomas practiced what he preached. When he expresses concern about those who compete with one another as to whose saint is the greatest, he is undoubtedly letting us glimpse some of the malaise of his time—the competition for honor and prestige among monasteries and convents. But he prefers to leave all honors and preferments to God.

When he talks about those who run about from shrine to shrine, he reflects the fascination for pilgrimage characteristic of his century. But he confesses that he has seldom "gone abroad," meaning outside the monastery, without returning home less a man than he was. And he observes that he sees little fruit or change for the better in the lives of those who busy themselves rushing about to see and hear new things.

When he talks about the need for repentance before God, we can hear the sorrow and grief of his own heart, as he reviews his own sin and unworthiness before the Holy of Holies.

So the book transcends its time, its geographical origins, even its author's individuality, and becomes a document for all times, speaking to the perennial human condition and dealing with the issues of our human need and the transforming power of Jesus Christ. Where others look for a different world, Thomas looks for a different self. His calling is to live each day in simple obedience to the Lord, and to pursue his daily tasks in the knowledge that only a changed heart can result in any lasting change for good. Some critics have criticized him as being essentially self-centered. They should look again at the profound and lasting influence this book has had over the past five hundred years. His words and thoughts have served as a stabilizing ballast for many others who have felt called to a more "active" life in the world and have plunged into the fray, to fight or work for change and progress in other ways.

The Imitation of Christ is a perpetual reminder that action—without humility and without a realistic sense of our human condition—will always in the long run be a "tale full of sound and fury, signifying nothing." On the other hand, this book should be an encouragement to those who seem destined to live out their lives in hidden, unnoticed places, with no great achievements to mark up to their credit, and no lasting fame to attach to their names.

NOTES

Notes for Book I of *The Confessions*

1. Note that the book begins with an ascription of praise. The word *Confessio* in St. Augustine's use has a wider meaning than the English *confession*, and includes ascriptions of praise as well as acknowledgment of sin.

   Throughout the *Confessions* Augustine uses an Old Latin version of the Old Testament, which he preferred even after he became acquainted with St. Jerome's new translation from the Hebrew (the Vulgate). He disapproved of the new translation, believing that the Greek Septuagint version of the Old Testament had been inspired, and that it was presumptuous for a single scholar to undertake such a revision.

2. Mortality is the evidence that God resists the proud—the penalty of that self-exaltation in which Augustine finds the ultimate motive of man's primary disobedience—aimed as setting self in the place of God.

3. Referring to St. Ambrose, who was then bishop of Milan.

Notes for Book I of *The Imitation of Christ*

4. *You have left the world* is used here to mean leaving the life of a layperson and entering a religious community.

5. Literally, *ad palmum pervenies*: to attain the palm.

6. Romans 12:2.

7. Psalm 37:3.

NOTES FOR BOOK II OF *The Imitation of Christ*

8. Luke 17:21.

9. Romans 14:17.

10. Psalm 45:13.

11. John 14:23.

12. John 12:34.

13. 1 Peter 5:7.

14. Hebrews 13:14.

15. Matthew 12:24, 16:21, 26:56.

16. 2 Timothy 2:5.

17. Romans 8:28.

18. James 3, Job 5:11.

19. Matthew 7:3.

20. Acts 22:3.

21. Galatians 6:2, 1 Corinthians 13:7.

22. Psalm 34:8.

23. Romans 1:20.

24. 1 Corinthians 1:31.

25. Wisdom 17:11.

26. Isaiah 57:21.

27. Luke 12:19.

28. Psalm 73:18–19.

29. 1 Samuel 16:7.

30. 2 Corinthians 10:18.

31. Isaiah 40:6.

32. John 11:28.

33. Matthew 16:26.

34. Romans 8:35.

35. Matthew 13:44.

36. Luke 12:21.

37. Proverbs 3:17.

38. Galatians 6:14.

39. Matthew 5:44, Luke 6:27–28.

40. Pope Sixtus II was martyred in Rome in AD 258. Six deacons were put to death with him. St. Lawrence, the seventh deacon, was killed four days later. These two men are among the most honored martyrs of Rome in the early centuries.

41. See Psalm 30:6–11.

42. John 3:8.

43. Job 7:18.

44. Luke 9:23.

45. Revelation 2:7.

46. James 1:17.

47. Matthew 22:21.

48. Luke 9:14, 22:41–42.

49. Philippians 2:21.

50. Matthew 26:24.

51. Luke 17:10, RSV.

52. Psalm 25:16.

53. Matthew 16:24.

54. Matthew 25:41.

55. Luke 14:27.

56. 2 Timothy 2:12, 1 Peter 4:13.

57. Luke 24:26.

58. 2 Corinthians 4:6, 11:23–30.

59. Matthew 20:23, John 18:11.

60. Romans 8:18.

61. Acts 9:16.

62. Acts 5:41.

63. Matthew 16:24.

64. Acts 16:2.

Notes for biography of St. Augustine

65. Pilkington, Rev. J. C., Translator. *The Confessions of St. Augustine*, 1876.

66. Gibb, John and William Montgomery, Editors. *The Confessions of Augustine* [Latin Version], Introduction. Cambridge University Press, 1927.

67. *Ibid.*

68. Augustine. *Epistle ccxxi.*

ABOUT PARACLETE PRESS

WHO WE ARE

Paraclete Press is a publisher of books, recordings, and DVDs on Christian spirituality. Our publishing represents a full expression of Christian belief and practice—from Catholic to Evangelical, from Protestant to Orthodox.

We are the publishing arm of the Community of Jesus, an ecumenical monastic community in the Benedictine tradition. As such, we are uniquely positioned in the marketplace without connection to a large corporation and with informal relationships to many branches and denominations of faith.

WHAT WE ARE DOING

Books

Paraclete publishes books that show the richness and depth of what it means to be Christian. Although Benedictine spirituality is at the heart of all that we do, we publish books that reflect the Christian experience across many cultures, time periods, and houses of worship. We publish books that nourish the vibrant life of the church and its people—books about spiritual practice, formation, history, ideas, and customs.

We have several different series, including the best-selling Paraclete Essentials and Paraclete Giants series of classic texts in contemporary English; Voices from the Monastery—men and women monastics writing about living a spiritual life today; award-winning poetry; best-selling gift books for children on the occasions of baptism and first communion; and the Active Prayer Series that brings creativity and liveliness to any life of prayer.

Recordings

From Gregorian chant to contemporary American choral works, our music recordings celebrate sacred choral music through the centuries. Paraclete distributes the recordings of the internationally acclaimed choir Gloriæ Dei Cantores, praised for their "rapt and fathomless spiritual intensity" by *American Record Guide*, and the Gloriæ Dei Cantores Schola, which specializes in the study and performance of Gregorian chant. Paraclete is also the exclusive North American distributor of the recordings of the Monastic Choir of St. Peter's Abbey in Solesmes, France, long considered to be a leading authority on Gregorian chant.

Videos

Our videos offer spiritual help, healing, and biblical guidance for life issues: grief and loss, marriage, forgiveness, anger management, facing death, and spiritual formation.

Learn more about us at our website: www.paracletepress.com, or call us toll-free at 1-800-451-5006.

 SCAN TO READ MORE

You may also be interested in these Paraclete Essentials . . .

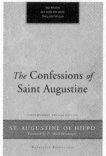

The Confessions of Saint Augustine
978-1-55725-695-9 | Trade paper, $16.99

The first autobiography ever written, Augustine's *Confessions* ranks among the most profound books in history. But it's more than that; this testament shows how God give rest to the weary and hope to the hopeless.

Little Talks with God
978-1-55725-779-6 | Trade paper, $15.99

While in an ecstatic trance, St. Catherine of Siena dictated *The Dialogue*. In this intense and searching work, she offers up petitions to God; fills her conversation with instruction on discernment, true and false spiritual emotion, obedience and truth; and reveals her famous image of Christ as the Bridge.

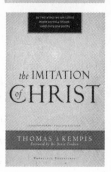

The Imitation of Christ
978-1-55725-608-9 | Trade paper, $15.99

The Imitation of Christ has enjoyed an unparalleled place in the world of books for more than five hundred years. At least 5000 different editions have been published, and it has been translated into almost every language in the world. Thomas à Kempis was a late medieval Catholic monk, a simple man who looked deeply into what it means to know God and have a relationship with Jesus.

You may also be interested in . . .

Three Ways of Loving God
St. Augustine, St. Teresa of Avila,
St. Francis de Sales

978-1-61261-499-1 | Trade paper, $13.99

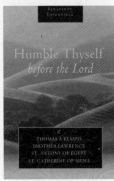

Humble Thyself Before the Lord
Thomas à Kempis, Br. Lawrence,
St. Antony of Egypt, St. Catherine of Siena

978-1-61261-503-5 | Trade paper, $11.99

These thematic collections of spiritual teachings from some of the best Christian writers in history are sure to be popular with book study groups, Centering prayer gatherings, adult Christian formation, and individual spiritual reading.